WorldView 4

D1709892

MICHAEL ROST

Araminta Crace   **Robin Wileman**
Antonia Clare   **JJ Wilson**

Simon Greenall
Series Editor, British English edition

Longman

WorldView Student Book 4

Authorized adaptation from the United Kingdom edition entitled *Language to Go*, First Edition, published by Pearson Education Limited publishing under its Longman imprint. Copyright © 2002 by Pearson Education Limited

American English adaptation: Ellen Shaw

American English adaptation published by Pearson Education, Inc. Copyright © 2005.

Pearson Education, 10 Bank Street, White Plains, NY 10606

Editorial director: Pamela Fishman
Development director: Irene Frankel
Senior development editor: José Antonio Méndez
Vice president, director of design and production: Rhea Banker
Executive managing editor: Linda Moser
Associate managing editors: Sandra Pike, Mike Kemper
Art director: Elizabeth Carlson
Vice president, director of international marketing: Bruno Paul
Senior manufacturing buyer: Edie Pullman
Text and cover design: Elizabeth Carlson
Photo research: Aerin Csigay
Text composition: Word and Image Design
Text font: 9.5/11pt Utopia and 9.5/11pt Frutiger Bold

ISBN: 0-13-184015-0

Library of Congress Control Number: 2003065959

Printed in the United States of America
3 4 5 6 7 8 9 10–BAM–09 08 07 06 05

Text Credits

Page **21** Somebody Already Broke My Heart. Words by Sade Adu. Music by Sade Adu, Stuart Matthewman, Andrew Hale, and Paul Spencer Denman. Copyright © 2000 Angel Music Ltd. All rights on behalf of Angel Music Ltd. in the United States administered by Sony/ATV Music Publishing, 8 Music Square West, Nashville, TN 37203. International copyright secured. All rights reserved; **59** Words Get in the Way by Gloria Estefan. Copyright © 2003 Foreign Imported Productions & Publishing, Inc. (BMI). International rights secured. All rights reserved. Used by permission; **97** Sad Songs (Say So Much). Words and music by Elton John and Bernie Taupin. Copyright © 1984 by Big Pig Music Ltd. All rights for the United States administered by Intersong U.S.A., Inc. International copyright secured. All rights reserved; **135** The Day Before You Came by Benny Goran, Bror Andersson, and Bjoern K. Ulvaeus. Copyright © 1983 Universal-Polygram International Publishing, Inc. on behalf of Union Songs Musikforlag AB. All rights reserved. Used by permission.

Illustration Credits

Steve Attoe, pp. 22, 24, 56, 62, 92; Pierre Berthiaume, p. 122; Brian Hughes, pp. 47, 93, 120, 130, 132; Paul McCusker, p. 36, 75, 80, 95, 100, 101; Susan Mogensen, p. 42; Steve Schulman, p. 74.

Photo Credits

Page **2** *(middle)* DigitalVision/PictureQuest, *(top left)* Chris Baker/Getty Images, *(top right)* SuperStock/PictureQuest, *(bottom left)* Robert Dowling/Corbis, *(bottom right)* Royalty-Free/Corbis; **3** Lawrence Manning; **4** Jerome Tisne/Getty Images; **6** Trevor Clifford, *(hat & umbrella)* Dorling Kindersley Media Library; **7** Trevor Clifford, *(water)* Eric Fowke/PhotoEdit, *(bottom)* Powerstock Zefa; **9** Ray Juno/Corbis; **11** *(top)* Warren Webb/PhotoLibrary.com, *(middle)* Dorling Kindersley Media Library, *(bottom)* Getty Images; **12** Pat LaCroix/Getty Images; **14** Trevor Clifford; **15** Trevor Clifford, *(F)* Dorling Kindersley Media Library, *(G)* Dorling Kindersley Media Library; **16** Greg Pease/Getty Images; **18** *(top left)* Ryan McVay/Getty Images, *(top middle)* Amos Morgan/Getty Images, *(top right)* Nicolas Russell/ Getty Images, *(right)* Willard Clay/Getty Images, *(bottom)* Mark Williams/Getty Images; **20** Eric Robert/Corbis; **25** M.Thomsen/ Masterfile; **26** *(top)* Doug Pensinger/Getty Images, *(middle)* The Granger Collection, *(bottom)* Frederick M. Brown/Getty Images; **27** *(top)* Trevor Clifford, *(bottom)* AP/Wide World Photos; **28** Britt Erlanson/Getty Images; **30** *(top left)* Dorling Kindersley Media Library, *(top right)* Getty Images, *(bottom left)* Royalty-Free/ Corbis, *(bottom right)* Frank La Bua/Pearson Education; **31** GDT; **32** Michael Newman/PhotoEdit; **34** *(A)* Adastra/Getty Images, *(B)* Dana White/PhotoEdit, *(C)* Christopher Bissell/Getty Images, *(D)* Stewart Cohen/Index Stock Imagery, *(E)* Dennis Nett/Syracuse Newspapers/The Image Works; *(F)* Susan Van Etten/PhotoEdit, *(G & H)* Spencer Grant/PhotoEdit, *(I & J)* Spencer Grant/PhotoEdit; **38** Rolex Awards/Tomas Bertelsen; **39** Matthew McVay/Corbis; **40** *(left)* Stockbyte/PictureQuest, *(right)* AP/Wide World Photos, *(bottom)* Warren Faidley/ ImageState; **41** Todd Bigelow/Aurora & Quanta Productions Inc.; **43** Rudi Von Briel/PhotoEdit; **46** Ronnie Kaufman/Corbis; **48** Gareth Boden; **49** Gareth Boden; **50** David Young-Wolff/ PhotoEdit; **54** *(top)* Britt Erlanson/Getty Images, *(bottom)* Getty Images; **58** Michael Putland/Retna Ltd.; **61** Kingfisher Challenges; **63** Digital Vision/Getty Images; **64** ImageState; **65** Katz Pictures/Antonio Pagnotta/Contrasto; **66** Robert Houser/Index Stock Imagery; **70** Marl Richards/PhotoEdit; **72** *(left)* Agency France Presse, *(top right)* Frank Trapper/Corbis, *(bottom right)* 20th Century Fox (courtesy Kobal); **73** Reuters/ Corbis; **75** *(top)* Roger Ressmeyer/Corbis, *(bottom left)* Corbis, *(bottom right)* Carlo Allegri/Getty Images; **76** Derek Trask/ Corbis; **77** AFP/Corbis; **78** Trevor Clifford; **79** Trevor Clifford; **82** Jurgen Schadeberg; **84** Roger Ressmeyer/Corbis; **89** Kevin Dodge/Masterfile; **90** *(A)* David Norton, *(B)* Eric Meola, *(C)* Oxford Scientific Films/Tony Tifford; **91** *(D)* Garden & Wildlife Matters/Martin P. Land, *(E)* Bruce Forster; **93** Dick Luria/Getty Images; **94** Susan Van Etten/PhotoEdit; **95** Photofest; **96** Tim Mosenfelder/Getty Images; **98** *(top)* SW Production/Index Stock Imagery, *(middle)* Gabe Palmer/Corbis, *(bottom)* Rob Melnychuk /Getty Images; **102** *(left)* Michael Newman/PhotoEdit, *(right)* Anthony Marsland; **104** Benelux Press/Index Stock Imagery; **106** *(A)* Powerstock Zefa, *(C)* David Young-Wolff/PhotoEdit, *(D)* Jeff Greenberg/PhotoEdit; **107** *(E)* M J Cardenas Productions/ Getty Images; **113** *(top)* Monika Graff/The Image Works, *(left)* Andy Sacks/Getty Images, *(right)* SW Productions/Getty Images; **114** Jeff Greenberg/PhotoEdit; **115** *(left)* Greer & Associates, Inc./SuperStock, *(middle)* Getty Images, *(right)* Pat LaCroix/Getty Images, **117** *(left)* Atlantic Syndication, *(right)* Trevor Clifford; **118** Jose Luis Pelaez, Inc./Corbis; **121** Lindsay Hebbard/Corbis; **127** Harvey Lloyd/Getty Images; **129** Charles O'Rear/NGS Image Collection; **133** Walter Stuart/Index Stock Imagery; **134** Carlos Alvarez/Getty Images.

Introduction

Welcome to *WorldView*, a four-level English course for adults and young adults. *WorldView* builds fluency by exploring a wide range of compelling topics presented from an international perspective. A trademark two-page lesson design, with clear and attainable language goals, ensures that students feel a sense of accomplishment and increased self-confidence in every class.

WorldView's approach to language learning follows a simple and proven **MAP**:
• **M**otivate learning through stimulating content and achievable learning goals.
• **A**nchor language production with strong, focused language presentations.
• **P**ersonalize learning through engaging and communicative speaking activities.

Course components

• **Student Book with Student Audio CD**
The Student Book contains 28 four-page units; seven Review Units (one after every four units); four World of Music Units (two in each half of the book); Information for Pair and Group Work; a Vocabulary list; and a Grammar Reference section.

The Student Audio CD includes tracks for all pronunciation and listening exercises in the *Student Book*. The Student Audio CD can be used with the *Student Book* for self-study and coordinates with the *Workbook* listening and pronunciation exercises.

• For each activity in the *Student Book*, the interleaved **Teacher's Edition** provides step-by-step procedures and exercise answer keys as well as a wealth of teacher support: unit Warm-ups, Optional Activities, Extensions, Culture Notes, Background Information, Teaching Tips, Wrap-ups, and extensive Language Notes. In addition, the *Teacher's Edition* includes a course orientation guide, full audio scripts, and the *Workbook* answer key.

• **The Workbook** has 28 four-page units that correspond to each of the *Student Book* units. Used in conjunction with the Student Audio CD, the *Workbook* provides abundant review and practice activities for Vocabulary, Grammar, Listening, Pronunciation, and Reading, along with Self-Quizzes after every four units. A Learning Strategies section at the beginning of the *Workbook* helps students to be active learners.

• **The Class Audio Program** is available in either CD or cassette format and contains all the recorded material for in-class use.

• **The Teacher's Resource Book** (with **Testing Audio CD** and **TestGen Software**) has three sections of reproducible material: extra communication activities for in-class use, model writing passages for each *Student Book* writing assignment, and a complete testing program: seven quizzes and two tests, along with scoring guides and answer keys. Also included are an Audio CD for use with the quizzes and tests and an easy-to-use TestGen software CD for customizing the tests.

• For each level of the course, the **WorldView Video** presents seven, five-minute authentic video segments connected to *Student Book* topics. Notes to the Teacher are available in the Video package, and Student Activity Sheets can be downloaded from the **WorldView Companion Website**.

• **The WorldView Companion Website** (www.longman.com/worldview) provides a variety of teaching support, including Video Activity Sheets and supplemental vocabulary material.

Unit contents

Each of the 28 units in *WorldView* has seven closely linked sections:
• **Getting started:** a communicative opening exercise that introduces target vocabulary
• **Listening:** an authentic-sounding conversation, radio interview, narration, etc., that introduces target grammar
• **Reading:** a magazine article, book excerpt, questionnaire, etc., that introduces target grammar
• **Grammar focus:** an exercise sequence that allows students to focus on the new grammar point and to solidify their learning
• **Pronunciation:** stress, rhythm, and intonation practice based on the target vocabulary and grammar
• **Speaking:** an interactive speaking task focused on student production of target vocabulary, grammar, and functional language
• **Writing:** a personalized writing activity that stimulates student production of target vocabulary and grammar
• **Conversation to go:** a concise reminder of the grammar and functional language introduced in the unit

Course length

With its flexible format and course components, *WorldView* responds to a variety of course needs, and is suitable for 70 to 90 hours of classroom instruction. Each unit can be easily expanded by using bonus activities from the *Teacher's Edition*, reproducible activities available in the *Teacher's Resource Book*, linked lessons from the *WorldView* Video program, and supplementary vocabulary assignments in the *WorldView* Companion Website.

The *WorldView Student Book* with Student Audio CD and the *Workbook* are also available in split editions.

Scope and Sequence

GRAMMAR FOCUS	PRONUNCIATION	SPEAKING	WRITING
Present perfect with *yet, already, just*	Falling and rising intonation in questions	Describing changes in your life	Write a letter about changes in your life
Real conditional	Stress in compound nouns	Making suggestions	Write an article for a travel magazine
Count/non-count nouns and quantifiers	Reduction of unstressed words	Describing how to make a dish	Write about what you eat on a typical day
Modals: *will, may, might, could* for prediction and speculation	Sentence stress: pitch changes around focus words	Making predictions about advances in technology	Describe a futuristic invention
Modals: *may, can, could, Is it OK if? / Do you mind if? / Would you mind if?* for permission	Intonation in polite requests	Asking for and giving/refusing permission	Write about polite customs and explain why they are important
Present perfect and present perfect continuous	Weak and contracted forms of *have* and *has*	Discussing personal achievements and ongoing activities	Write an application letter
Expressions of purpose: *to, in order to, so that, for*	Stress patterns in words	Describing reasons for doing things	Write an email about security measures in the workplace and their consequences
Past perfect	Weak and contracted forms of *had*	Talking about events in your life	Describe an interesting experience
Indirect statements	The *th* sounds: /ð/ (weather) and /θ/ (thick)	Reporting on what you hear or read	Write an email describing the weather and making predictions
Simple future and future perfect	Contracted and weak forms of *will* and *have*	Predicting future events	Write a diary entry about future plans
Indirect questions	Consonant clusters	Reporting a conversation or interview	Write a letter recounting a conversation or interview
Narrative past tenses: simple past, past continuous, past perfect, past perfect continuous	Main stress in sentences	Telling stories in the past	Write a story about important events in your past
Present unreal conditional	Weak and contracted forms of *would* and weak pronunciation of *could*	Talking about hypothetical situations	Write about an extreme, hypothetical situation
Connectors: *although, despite (not), however, in spite of*	Phrase groups and intonation	Comparing attitudes toward life situations	Describe daily routines related to commuting

Lesson A

Changes

Vocabulary Words related to lifestyles
Grammar Present perfect with *yet, already, just*
Speaking Describing changes in your life

Getting started

1 **Which of these do you have in your life right now? Check (✓) them.**

clutter ____	contentment ____	energy ____
good health ____	good luck ____	happiness ____
productivity ____	stress ____	success ____
tension ____	tranquility ____	wealth ____

2 *PAIRS.* **Answer these questions about the things in Exercise 1.**

Which things would you like to have more of or less of?
Which are the three most important things for you?
Can we do anything to change things? If so, what can we do?

3 *PAIRS.* **Write the adjective form for the nouns in Exercise 1.**

clutter—cluttered

4 🎧 **Listen and check your answers. Then listen and repeat.**

2

Reading

5 Have you ever heard of Feng Shui? Where do you think it comes from?

6 Read the article about Feng Shui and answer these questions.

1. What does the article say you should do every day?
2. What does the article say about colors?

Want to change your life but don't know how?

Is Feng Shui the answer?

Feng Shui is an ancient Chinese philosophy for a healthy, happy, and successful lifestyle that will make you more content with your life. Read on for some advice.

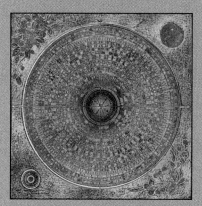
Chart used for setting up Feng Shui.

- Take up a sport or start going for a walk every day. Make sure you get some fresh air during the day.
- Start your day with a glass of water. You'll feel more energetic.
- Buy a fish tank. Fish are considered lucky, so you may even become wealthy!
- Clean up your home and workplace every day.
- Use plants to create a calm and tranquil atmosphere at home or at work.
- Don't wear gray clothes. Gray is neither black nor white; it's a sign of confusion.
- Try to avoid stressful or tense situations and places, like crowded streets and noisy traffic.

Remember: With Feng Shui, you don't predict the future. You change it.

7 *PAIRS.* Discuss. Do you think Feng Shui works? Would you like to try it?

Listening

8 Listen to the interview with Bill Costa, who has tried Feng Shui. In the article on Feng Shui, check (✓) the advice that Bill has followed.

9 Listen again. Write *T* (true) or *F* (false) after each statement.

1. Feng Shui has changed Bill's life.
2. Bill has started running recently.
3. He believes that the fish have brought him good luck.

1

Lesson B

Grammar focus

1 **Study the examples of the present perfect with *yet*, *already*, and *just*.**

> **Have** you **bought** any fish **yet**?
> I **haven't started** on the house **yet**.
> I**'ve tried** one or two of the ideas **already**.
> I**'ve already cleaned** up my desk.
> I**'ve just bought** myself a new blue suit.

2 **Look at the examples again. Complete the rules in the chart with *yet*, *already*, or *just*.**

Present perfect with *yet*, *already*, and *just*
Use _____ when something hasn't happened, but you expect it to happen in the future.
Use _____ when something has happened very recently.
Use _____ when something has happened sooner than expected.
Use _____ in questions and negative sentences.
_____ always goes between *have* and the past participle.
_____ goes at the end of a clause.
_____ can go either between *have* and the past participle or at the end of the clause.

> *Grammar Reference page 142*

3 **Write sentences in the present perfect using the cues. Use *yet*, *already*, and *just* where appropriate.**

1. My neighbor works out every day. (She / start training for the marathon)

   She's just started training for the marathon.

2. Kumiko works really fast. (She / do her homework)

3. What's the weather like this morning? (You / be outside?)

4. (My neighbor / redecorate / his living room) It looks great!

5. I don't know where I'm going on vacation. (I / not decided)

6. (I / finish reading a book on Feng Shui) It's very interesting.

7. Rogelio had to be home early today. (He / leave)

8. I don't want to watch that movie on TV. (I / see it)

9. Are you hungry? (You / have lunch?)

10. I'm so happy. (I / find a job) I start next week.

Pronunciation

4 🎧 **Listen. Notice the way the intonation changes on the focus word (the most important word). The intonation then goes up at the end of the *Yes/No* questions and down at the end of the *Wh-* questions.**

Has your life **changed** yet?   What **chang**es have you made in your life?

How about straightening up your **work**place?   Have you bought any **fish** yet?

5 🎧 **Listen again and repeat.**

Speaking

6 *BEFORE YOU SPEAK.* **Think about recent changes in your life—in your home, work, family, leisure activities, or personal appearance. Make notes on two or three changes you have already made, and one or two changes you plan to make.**

Already done	Not done yet
joined a gym	started working out

7 *GROUPS OF 4.* **Take turns. Ask each other questions about the changes in your lives.**

A: *What changes have you made in your life recently?*
B: *Well, I've just joined a gym.*
C: *Really? And how often do you go?*

Writing

8 **Write a short letter to a friend. Tell your friend about recent changes in your life. What have you done and what haven't you done yet to make these changes?**

CONVERSATION TO GO

A: **Have** you **finished** moving in **yet**?
B: No, Mother, we just got here. We **haven't unpacked** a thing **yet**! No, you can't come for dinner!

Australia

Vocabulary Travel items
Grammar Real conditional
Speaking Making suggestions

A___
B___
C___
D___

Lesson A

Getting started

1 *PAIRS.* **Think of things you might take on a camping trip. Match the words on the left with the words on the right to make compound nouns.**

1. first-aid _kit_	gear
2. hiking _____	guide
3. insect _____	belt
4. money _____	bottle
5. rain _____	bag
6. sleeping _____	boots
7. travel _____	repellent
8. water _____	~~kit~~

2 **Look at the pictures of the travel items. Label them with the words in Exercise 1.**

Pronunciation

3 🎧 **Listen to the words in Exercise 1. Which syllable is stressed in a compound noun?**

4 🎧 **Listen again and repeat.**

5 *PAIRS* **Which of the travel items from Exercise 1 would you take on a . . .**

- two-week vacation at the beach?
- trip to the mountains?
- weekend visit to a big city?

6

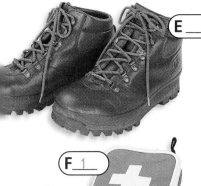

E___

F_1_

Listening

6 🎧 **Jeff is packing for a weekend trip. Listen to his conversation with his roommate. Look at the pictures and check (✓) the things Jeff is taking.**

Reading

7 **Look at the picture of the Australian Outback and answer these questions.**

Do you know anyone who has been to Australia?

What do you know about it?

G___

8 **Read the article about the Australian Outback and answer these questions.**

1. What's the best way to travel around the Outback?
2. When is the best time to go?
3. What wildlife can you see?
4. What outdoor activities are there?
5. What health risks are there?

H___

9 *PAIRS.* **Compare your answers.**

The Australian Outback

The Outback is huge—it's 1,878 miles (3,022 km) from Adelaide to Darwin. So, unless you have a lot of time, you'll find that flights and rental cars are the best ways to travel. It will be cheaper to buy a pass if you plan to take several flights.

Unless you like extremely hot weather, avoid December and January, when the temperature can go up to 40°C (104°F). If you go in July and August, it won't be too hot during the day, but the nights will be freezing. The best times to visit are April to June and October to November. If you visit Kakadu's wetlands in the dry season, you'll see thousands of crocodiles.

And if you want to see kangaroos, look for them in the mornings and evenings. You may even see dingoes—if you're very lucky.

If you like outdoor activities, you can go canoeing up Katherine Gorge or ride camels at Uluru. One of the best ways to see the Outback is to walk. Wear boots if you go walking—Australia has the most dangerous snakes in the world. The sun is very strong for most of the year, so you should use high-SPF sunscreen and wear a hat. You should also carry plenty of water with you. If you want to go camping, you'll find that many tour companies offer camping trips.

Grammar focus

1 Study the examples of the real conditional. Notice that each sentence has two parts: an *if* clause and a result clause.

> It **will be** cheaper to buy a pass **if** you **plan** to take several flights.
> **If** you**'re going** hiking, you**'ll need** some insect repellent.
> **If** you **like** outdoor activities, you **can go** canoeing up Katherine Gorge.
> **If** you **go** in July or August, it **won't be** too hot.
> **Unless** you **like** extremely hot weather, **avoid** December and January.

2 Look at the examples again. Complete the rules in the chart with *if* or *result*.

Real conditional
Use the real conditional to talk about future possibilities.
The _____ clause states the condition.
Use the simple present tense in the _____ clause.
Use the future with *will* or *be going to*, a modal, or an imperative in the _____ clause.
NOTE: *Unless* can sometimes be used in place of *if . . . not*.

Grammar Reference page 142

3 Combine the beginnings of the sentences on the left with the endings on the right to make conditional sentences. Use *if* or *unless* as appropriate.

Take a water bottle if you want safe drinking water.

1. Take a water bottle
2. You'll need to wear boots
3. You may see fantastic sunrises
4. You'll need to take rain gear
5. Find a tour company offering adventure sports
6. You'll need to use sunscreen
7. You may not get tickets for the flights
8. You'll get lost

a. you make your reservations in advance.
b. you don't want to get sunburned.
c. you want to go canoeing.
d. you go hiking.
e. you use a very good map.
f. you want safe drinking water.
g. you go in the dry season.
h. you get up early.

Speaking

4 *BEFORE YOU SPEAK.* **Think about a tourist destination in your country or any place you know. Make notes about your chosen place.**

Tourist destination

The best time to go

The weather

Clothes to bring

Tourist activities and attractions

Health risks

5 *PAIRS.* **Role-play. Student A, you're a travel agent giving suggestions and information to Student B. Student B, you're a tourist. You want to go to the place Student A chose in Exercise 4. Ask Student A questions about the place. Then switch roles.**

B: Hi. I'd like some information about British Columbia, Canada.
A: Sure. What do you want to know?
B: When is the best time to go there?
A: If you go in June, you'll have very nice weather.

6 **Report to the class. What have you learned about the place your partner chose?**

Writing

7 **Write a short article for a travel magazine describing a vacation place that you know. Use the real conditional.**

CONVERSATION TO GO

A: When is the best time to go?
B: If you go in the winter, you'll avoid the crowds.

What's cooking?

Vocabulary Cooking terms and ingredients
Grammar Count/non-count nouns and quantifiers
Speaking Describing how to make a dish

Lesson A

Getting started

1 *PAIRS.* **Discuss these questions.**

How often do you cook?
What is your favorite type of food?

2 *PAIRS.* **Match the words in the box with their definitions.**

a. add	b. (bring to a) boil	c. broil	d. chop	e. melt	f. mix
g. pour	h. sauté	i. serve	j. simmer	k. soak	l. stir

1. Put one ingredient in with another ___a___
2. Cook quickly in a little hot oil or fat ____
3. Turn solid food into liquid by heating it ____
4. Present a finished meal, ready for eating ____
5. Cook in very hot water ____
6. Cover with liquid for a period of time ____

7. Cut into small uneven pieces ____
8. Combine different ingredients together ____
9. Cook meat, fish, etc., over or under direct heat ____
10. Move a liquid or food with a spoon in order to mix it ____
11. Cook slowly in liquid over low heat ____
12. Make liquid flow steadily from a container ____

Listening

3 🎧 **Listen to the cooking show, *Now We're Cooking*, and look at the pictures. Which group of ingredients is for the first recipe?**

A

B

10

4 🎧 **Listen to the chef's recipes and complete the sentences.**

Chile con carne

1. Boil the _kidney beans_ for 10 minutes.

2. _____ the onions and the beef until the beef turns brown.

3. Add the tomato paste, the chopped _____, and the kidney beans.

4. Let the chili con carne _____ for 30 minutes.

5. _____ with rice.

Cajun shrimp

1. Let the sauce _____ for about an hour.

2. _____ most of the butter in a large saucepan.

3. Cook the _____ for 2 minutes, before adding the rest of the butter.

4. Add the rest of the butter and the _____.

5. Serve with _____.

Reading

5 **Have you ever heard of the Mediterranean diet? What do you think it is?**

6 **Read the article. Complete the chart to describe what people eat on the Mediterranean diet.**

7 *PAIRS.* **Discuss these questions.**

Is your diet similar to the Mediterranean diet, or is it very different?

Do you think you would like the Mediterranean diet? Why?

A little	red meat
A lot	
Some	

The Mediterranean Diet

The Mediterranean diet comes from a number of different countries bordering the Mediterranean Sea, including Greece, southern Italy, Portugal, and southern Spain. People who follow this diet generally live longer, and very few get heart disease.

Mediterranean people eat a lot of fruit, vegetables, grains, beans, and nuts on a regular basis. They use a great deal of olive oil. They don't eat much butter, but they do have some dairy products, including milk. People from this region eat fish and poultry a few times a week. However, the diet does not include a great deal of red meat. People from the Mediterranean region also drink a small amount of wine with a meal, which according to several studies, has some health benefits.

Many people in non-Mediterranean countries have switched to the Mediterranean diet because it is not only a healthful way of eating, but an enjoyable one.

3

Grammar focus

1 Look at the examples. Are the words in italics count or non-count nouns? Write *C* or *NC* next to each sentence. Notice the quantifiers before count and non-count nouns.

> Heat a little *oil* in a saucepan.
> Chop several *onions*.

2 Look at the examples again and the article on page 11. Write the quantifiers in the correct columns in the chart.

a few	all	most of	a great deal of	a lot of
much	a number of	each	plenty of	a little
few	some	a little bit of	many	several

Count/Non-count nouns and quantifiers		
Count nouns only	**Non-count nouns only**	**Both**
a few		

Grammar Reference page 142

3 Underline the correct quantifiers.

1. <u>**a few**</u> / **a little** herbs
2. **each / all** the onions
3. **a little / a few** salt and pepper
4. **a lot of / several** tomato paste
5. **most of / many of** the butter
6. **a large number of / plenty of** vegetable oil
7. **several / some** chili powder
8. **a little bit of / a few** chicken stock
9. **a little / a small number of** chili powder
10. **not too many / not too much** milk
11. **not a great deal of / not a large number of** chili powder
12. **much / several** eggs

Pronunciation

4 🎧 **Listen. Notice the pronunciation of the words** *a*, *and*, *of*, *in*, **and** *some*.
Are these words stressed? Why?

a clove of garlic   Chop a clove of garlic.

some oil   Heat some oil in a pan.

salt and pepper   Add a little salt and pepper.

a lot of   Don't use a lot of chili powder.

5 🎧 **Listen again and repeat.**

Speaking

6 *BEFORE YOU SPEAK.* **Think of a dish**
you know how to cook. Make notes on the
ingredients and procedure for cooking.

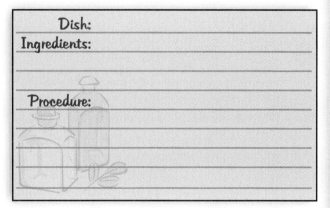

Dish:
Ingredients:

Procedure:

7 *PAIRS.* **Take turns explaining how to make**
your dish. Ask and answer questions about
ingredients and procedures. Take notes on
your partner's recipe.

A: *For this pasta dish, we need macaroni,*
chicken stock, onions, tomatoes . . .

B: *How much macaroni do we need?*

A: *One box of macaroni and a lot of chicken stock—*
about four cups. We need several onions and tomatoes . . .

8 **Tell the class about your partner's dish. Would you like to try it?**

Writing

9 **Write about what you eat on a typical day. Be as specific as you can.**
As appropriate, use quantifiers with count and non-count nouns.

CONVERSATION TO GO

A: What ingredients will I need to make this dish?
B: Several large eggs, some butter, a little bit of garlic, and a little salt.

UNIT 4

Toys of the future

Vocabulary   Toys and games
Grammar   Modals: *will, may, might, could*
for prediction and speculation
Speaking   Making predictions

Getting started

1 *PAIRS.* **Match the words in the box with the pictures.**

1. action figure *C*
2. board game ____
3. cards ____
4. doll ____
5. erector set truck ____
6. handheld video game ____
7. jigsaw puzzle ____
8. remote-controlled car ____
9. skateboard ____
10. stuffed animal ____

2 *PAIRS.* **Discuss these questions.**

Which toys and games did you play with when you were a child?

Which toys and games are popular with adults?

What kinds of toys and games do you think will be popular in the future?

Listening

3 🎧 **Listen to the radio interview. Which of the following are discussed in the interview? Circle the letters.**

a. dolls
b. virtual child
c. toy robots
d. emotionally sensitive toys

4 🎧 **Listen again. Answer the questions. Use the choices in Exercise 3.**

1. Which toy will be able to create a computer image of a real toy?
2. Which toys will be able to tell your mood?
3. Which toys will be able to talk to people?

5 *PAIRS.* **Discuss. Do you think the dolls of the future might be good for children? Why?**

Tomorrow's Toys

In the future, toys will give us excitement, entertainment, and wonderful learning opportunities. What kinds of toys can we expect to see?

Reading

6 Look at the article "Tomorrow's Toys." Look at the names of the six toys. Without reading the descriptions, guess what these toys will be like.

7 Read the article quickly to see if your guesses in Exercise 6 were correct.

8 Read the article again. Write *T* (true) or *F* (false) after each statement.

1. Some toys will protect children from traffic dangers. T
2. Some toys will talk to people.
3. Some toys will teach people new languages.
4. Ludic Robots® will be able to follow some orders.
5. Soccer balls of the future might cause arguments.
6. The hover skateboard will move on wheels.

E

F

G

H

I

J

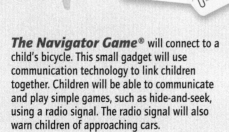

The Navigator Game® will connect to a child's bicycle. This small gadget will use communication technology to link children together. Children will be able to communicate and play simple games, such as hide-and-seek, using a radio signal. The radio signal will also warn children of approaching cars.

Ludic Robots® are small, electronic friends that respond to voice commands, touch, and gestures. They can also be taught to do simple tasks, so children may become very fond of them.

Soccer balls of the future might contain video cameras. These cameras could show exactly where the ball is, so arguments about goals might become a thing of the past.

The Interactive Globe® will show lots of information about the world, such as different time zones, the world's languages, and the weather around the world. When not in use, the Globe could be used as a night-light.

Interactive Books® will grow up with their readers, taking them from simple story-telling with pictures through learning to read. Readers will use a touch screen to choose voices and faces for their characters and create their own pictures, making the stories more personal.

The hover skateboard could become available in a few years. It will look almost like a regular skateboard, but instead of moving on wheels, it will glide on a cushion of air.

Lesson B

Grammar focus

1 Study the examples with *will, may, might,* and *could* for prediction and speculation.

> I'm sure little girls **will** still play with dolls.
> Children **may** become very fond of the Ludic Robots.
> The Globe **could** be used as a night-light.
> I think some children **might** want a virtual friend.

2 Look at the examples again. Complete the rules in the chart with *will, may, might,* or *could.*

> **Modals:** *will, may, might, could* for prediction and speculation
>
> Use _____ to express a future event that is very likely to happen.
>
> Use _____ , _____ , and _____ to express a future event that is possible, but less likely, to happen.
>
> ---
> **NOTE:** Use *will, may, might,* or *could* after *I think.* Use *will* after *I'm sure,*
> *I don't think / I doubt if, I expect.*

Grammar Reference page 143

3 Write sentences about the future using the cues. Use *will, may, might, could,* or *won't.*
Some items may have more than one answer.

1. I think / computer graphics / become / very realistic (very likely)

   I think computer graphics will become very realistic.

2. In the future / more children / play indoors / all the time (possibly)

3. I'm sure / people / not read / printed books much longer (very likely)

4. Personal flying machines / become / available / by the year 2020 (possibly)

5. I expect / most children / have / cell phones and pagers / before long (very likely)

6. Very soon / I think / famous people / be / characters in computer games (very likely)

7. Skateboards / have / electric motors / soon (possibly)

8. I expect / stuffed animals / not be / very popular much longer (very likely)

9. Digitally created characters / replace human actors in movies (possibly)

4 *GROUPS OF 3.* Which of the sentences in Exercise 3 do you agree with?

Pronunciation

5 🎧 Long sentences are often divided into thought groups. Listen. Notice the way the focus word (the most important word) in each sentence or thought group stands out. The voice jumps up or down on this word and the vowel sound is long and clear.

I'm **sure** / little girls will play with **dolls**./   I ex**pect** / they'll have dis**cus**sions with their dolls. /

Do you **real**ly think/ dolls will **talk** to people?/   I'm **sure** they will. /

Do you **think** / this could happen anytime **soon**?/   It **might** happen / sooner than we **think**. /

6 🎧 Listen again and repeat.

Speaking

7 *BEFORE YOU SPEAK.* Think about these kinds of products. What do you think they will be like in the future? Make notes about your predictions.

> Toys   small, have computers in them
>
> Video and computer games
>
> Other kinds of technology

8 *PAIRS.* Take turns asking and answering questions about your predictions. Use these expressions in your answers:

• I think   • I don't think   • I expect   • I doubt if   • I'm sure

A: *What do you think the toys of the future will be like?*
B: *I'm sure that a lot of toys will have computers in them.*

Writing

9 Think of a product for the future that you'd like to have, for example, a toy, an appliance, or a car. Write a description of this product for a catalog.

CONVERSATION TO GO

A: Do you think life will get better in the future?
B: I can't say, but I know it'll be different!

Unit 1 Changes

1 🎧 *PAIRS.* Listen to three people talking about changes they are making in their lives. Discuss what each person has done so far and what he or she plans to do.

A Roberto

B Tao

C Alex

2 *PAIRS.* Choose one of these projects or another project of your own. Tell your partner. Your partner will ask questions about what you have done to reach your goals. Take turns.

- clean up or redecorate the house
- get a good (or better) job
- get in shape

- improve your English
- play a sport really well
- find a boyfriend/girlfriend

Unit 2 Australia

3 *PAIRS.* Look at the pictures and discuss these questions.

Have you ever been to these places?
What do you know about them?
Would you like to go to either one?

4 *PAIRS.* Role-play a travel agent and a traveler who wants to visit one of the places in the pictures. Ask and answer questions. Then switch roles.

Student A, look at page 136.
Student B, look at page 138.

Colorado, USA

Bangkok, Thailand

Unit 3 What's cooking?

5 *PAIRS.* Look at a recipe for one minute and try to remember the ingredients and procedure. Don't look at your partner's recipe.

Student A, look at page 136. Student B, look at page 138.

6 *PAIRS.* Take turns telling your partner how to make your "dish" but don't say what it is. Your partner guesses what it is. Ask and answer follow-up questions.

A: *First break some eggs.*
B: *How many?*

7 *PAIRS.* Follow the same directions from Exercise 6 for another recipe that you know how to prepare.

Unit 4 Toys of the future

8 Listen to the radio interview with a futurologist. Do you agree with his predictions?

9 *GROUPS OF 4.* Make predictions as a group for changes you think will or might happen 20 years in the future. Discuss the following ideas and others of your own.

Topic	Possibilities	Agree or Disagree?
Money	Electronic cash? World currency?	
Electronic shopping	Everyone will use it? Some won't?	
TVs/video	Video walls? 3-D TVs and video games?	
Robots	Will do all the housework? Might be lovable?	
Energy	Will cost more? Could cost less?	
Other ideas		

10 Share your opinions with the rest of the class.

World of Music *1*

Somebody Already Broke My Heart

Sade

Vocabulary

1 Match the words in bold with the correct definitions.

1. My friends are always there to **pull** me **through** a crisis. _c_

2. It **tears** me **apart** when I see someone in pain.

3. I can always **count on** my family to help me. ___

4. I was once **stranded** at the airport without any money. ___

5. We all need a **savior** at some point in our lives. ___

a. depend or rely on something or someone

b. needing help because you are unable to move from a place or situation

c. help someone survive after a difficult or upsetting situation

d. someone or something that saves you from a difficult situation

e. make someone extremely unhappy or upset

*Born Helen Folasade Adu in 1959, pop and rock star **Sade** spent her early years in Nigeria and then moved to England. She started in the music world as a songwriter to later become a singer. Her hits include "Smooth Operator" and "Love Is Stronger Than Pride."*

2 *PAIRS.* **Choose one verb or verb phrase from Exercise 1 to talk about a personal experience.**

Listening

3 Listen to "Somebody Already Broke My Heart" by Sade. How does the singer feel? Circle the answer.

a. She has found someone to love, but she's afraid of being hurt again.

b. She doesn't want to fall in love ever again.

c. She is afraid that she will hurt the new person in her life.

4 Listen to the song again and complete the lyrics on page 21.

20

Somebody Already Broke My Heart

You came along when I needed a savior

Someone to pull me through somehow

____ ____ ____ apart so many times

____ ____ ____ so many times before

So I'm counting on you now

Somebody already broke my heart

Somebody already broke my heart

Here I am

So don't leave me stranded

On the end of a line

Hanging on the edge of a lie

____ ____ ____ apart so many times

____ ____ ____ so many times before

So be careful and be kind

Somebody already broke my heart

If someone ____ ____ lose,

  I ____ ____ ____ play

Somebody already broke my heart

No, no I can't go there again

You came along when I needed a savior

Someone to pull me through somehow

____ ____ ____ apart so many times

____ ____ ____ so many times before

So I'm counting on you now

Somebody already broke my heart

If someone ____ ____ lose,

  I ____ ____ ____ play

Somebody already broke my heart

No, no I can't go there again

Speaking

5 *GROUPS OF 3.* **Discuss these questions. Use lines from the song to explain your answers.**

1. Look at the first stanza. The singer says she needed a "savior." Why did she need to be saved?

2. How does the singer ask the new person in her life to behave?

UNIT 5

How rude!

Vocabulary Manners and polite customs
Grammar Modals: *may, can, could,* and *Is it OK if . . . ?/Do you mind if . . . ?/*
Would you mind if . . . ? for permission
Speaking Asking for and giving/refusing permission

Getting started

1 *PAIRS.* **Look at the picture and answer these questions.**

1. Who is snapping his/her fingers? B
2. Who has his/her elbows on the table?
3. Who is slurping while eating?
4. Who is reaching across the table?
5. Who is pointing at someone?
6. Who is eating with his or her fingers?
7. Who is blowing his or her nose?
8. Who has his or her feet up on the chair?

2 *GROUPS OF 3.* **Discuss. Which of the behaviors in the picture are rude in your country?**

Reading

3 *PAIRS.* **How much do you know about good manners in the United States? Take the quiz. Check (✓) *T* (true) or *F* (false) after each statement.**

Minding Your Manners

> Did you know that good manners are cultural? In other words, what's all right to do in one country may not be appropriate in another country. See how much you know about what's OK and what's not OK in the United States.

in the United States

	T	F
1. It's impolite to ask people how much money they make.	○	○
2. It's OK to interrupt other people while they are talking.	○	○
3. When someone invites you to a restaurant, it's OK to offer to pay for your meal.	○	○
4. It's impolite to put your elbows on the table at mealtimes.	○	○
5. When people invite you to their house for dinner, it's impolite to be a few minutes early.	○	○
6. When you are at a friend's house, it's OK to use your friend's telephone without asking.	○	○
7. In a restaurant, it's OK to snap your fingers when you want to call the server.	○	○
8. It's very rude to eat when you are walking down the street.	○	○
9. It's impolite to point your finger at another person.	○	○
10. It's impolite to smoke in a public place without asking.	○	○
11. It's impolite to open a present in front of the person who gave it to you.	○	○
12. It's very rude to give money as a wedding present.	○	○

Check your answers on page 140.

4 *GROUPS OF 4.* **Were you surprised by any of the answers? Are the answers the same for your country?**

Listening

5 🎧 **Listen and match the conversations with the general situations described in the quiz in Exercise 3.**

a. _6_   b. _____   c. _____   d. _____   e. _____   f. _____   g. _____

Grammar focus

1 Study the examples. Notice the ways to ask for permission and the ways to respond.

Asking permission	Giving permission	Refusing permission
May I take care of the tip? **Can** I pay for my share?	Sure. Why not?	**Oh, no.** You're my guest.
Could I use your phone, please?	Yes, of course.	**Sorry, but** I'm expecting a call.
Is it OK if I use the fax?	Sure, go ahead.	**No, sorry.** It's not working right now.
Do you mind if I smoke?	No, I don't mind.	**I'm sorry, but** smoking is not allowed.
Would you mind if sat here?	No, not at all.	**I'm sorry, but** this seat is taken.

2 Look at the examples again. Underline the correct information to complete the rules in the chart.

> **Modals: *may, can, could,* and *Is it OK if . . . ? / Do you mind if . . . ? / Would you mind if . . . ?* for permission**
>
> After *may, can,* and *could*, use the **base form of the verb / infinitive**.
>
> After *Is it OK if* + subject and *Do you mind if* + subject, use the **base form / simple present form** of the verb.
>
> After *Would you mind if* + subject, use the **simple present / simple past** form of the verb.
>
> To give permission to questions beginning with *Do you mind* or *Would you mind*, say **yes / no**.

Grammar Reference page 143

3 Write conversations using the cues. Be sure to give a reason when you refuse.

1. A: I want to open the window. (do/mind)
   B: (agree)

   A: Do you mind if I open the window?
   B: No, not at all.

2. A: I want to give you some advice. (may)
   B: (agree)

3. A: I'd like to use your pencil. (could)
   B: (agree)

4. A: I need to borrow your dictionary. (can)
   B: (refuse)

5. A: We want to sit here. (OK)
   B: (refuse)

6. A: I'd like to use your computer. (would/mind)
   B: (agree)

7. A: I'd like to call you sometime. (could)
   B: (agree)

8. A: I want to leave work early today. (would/mind)
   B: (refuse)

Pronunciation

4 🎧 Listen. Notice the rising intonation in these polite questions.

May we have the **check**, please?   Is it OK if I leave **ear**ly?

Do you mind if I come **in**?   Would you mind if I asked you a **ques**tion?

5 🎧 Listen to these questions. You will hear each question twice. Which intonation sounds more polite, *a* or *b*?

1. Could I use your phone? ____

2. Is it OK if I close the window? ____

3. Do you mind if I sit here? ____

4. Can I look at your newspaper? ____

6 🎧 Listen and repeat the polite questions.

Speaking

7 *PAIRS.* Take turns asking for permission and responding.

Student A: look at page 139. Read the situations.
Student B: look at page 141. Respond to Student A.

A: Can I use your computer?
B: I'm sorry, but I need it to do my homework.

8 Switch roles.

Student B: look at page 141. Read the situations.
Student A: look at page 139. Respond to Student B.

Writing

9 Think of two or three important polite ways in your country for making requests or asking permission. Describe what those customs mean and explain why it is important to use them in your culture.

CONVERSATION TO GO

A: **Could I borrow** your car?
B: **I'm sorry.** I need it tonight.
A: Well, **is it OK if I use your phone** to call a taxi?

UNIT 6

Achievement

Vocabulary Verbs related to achievements and projects
Grammar Present perfect and present perfect continuous
Speaking Discussing personal achievements and projects

Lesson A

Getting started

1 **PAIRS.** Match the verbs with the correct nouns to make expressions related to achievements.

Verbs	Nouns
1. achieve _f_	a. an obstacle / a problem
2. come up with _g_	b. a certificate / an award
3. develop ___	c. a race / a prize
4. invent ___	d. a skill / a plan
5. overcome ___	e. a machine / a device
6. pass ___	f. a goal / an objective
7. receive ___	g. an idea / a solution
8. solve ___	h. an exam / a course
9. win ___	i. a problem / a puzzle

2 **PAIRS.** Complete the sentences with the correct form of the verbs in Exercise 1. You will not need all the verbs.

1. Lance Armstrong tied the Tour de France record when he _____won_____ the race for the fifth time.

2. Albert Einstein _____ the theory of relativity, an idea that changed physics forever.

3. After she left Destiny's Child, Beyonce _____ numerous awards, including five Grammies in 2004.

4. Airline pilots have to _____ rigorous exams to keep their jobs.

5. After many years of hard work, David Beckham _____ his goal of becoming a soccer star.

6. Of all the devices that people have ever _____, the steam engine is the most far-reaching.

7. Imagination is the capacity to _____ a problem you have never had before.

3 **GROUPS OF 4.** Choose two phrases from Exercise 1. Make sentences about yourself or people you know. Take turns sharing your sentence. Ask and answer follow-up questions.

My friend at work came up with a great idea for a new video game.

Listening

4 🎧 Listen to the radio program about Trevor Baylis, an inventor. Which of the three radios did Trevor Baylis invent? Check (✓) the correct picture.

5 🎧 Listen again and answer these questions.

1. Why did Trevor invent the windup radio?
2. What else has he invented?
3. What is he working on and developing currently?

A___

B___

C___

Reading

6 Look at the picture of a new invention called the IBOT™. What do you think it will be able to do?

7 Read the article. Was your answer in Exercise 6 correct?

8 Read the article again and answer these questions.

1. How is the IBOT different from ordinary wheelchairs?
2. Why did Kamen come up with the idea of improving the wheelchair?
3. How did he start to develop the technology for his invention?
4. What makes him want to work on a new project?

REINVENTING THE WHEELCHAIR

Have you ever heard the phrase "confined to a wheelchair"? The phrase is often used to refer to people using wheelchairs. But inventor Dean Kamen thinks wheelchairs should help physically impaired people become free. He has come up with a design for a revolutionary new wheelchair called the IBOT™, or the Independence IBOT™ Mobility System.

Kamen's invention promises to improve the way many people live. The IBOT™ will go almost anywhere, climb up and down stairs, and even raise itself up to reach top shelves.

For years, Kamen has been working on projects to make people's lives better. He says, "I don't work on a project unless I believe that it will dramatically improve life for a bunch of people."

How did Kamen come up with the idea for the IBOT™? Years ago, he noticed a young man in the street unsuccessfully trying to get his wheelchair onto a curb. Kamen started thinking about how to improve the wheelchair. Then, one day, while he was stepping out of the shower, he slipped. To regain his balance, he swiveled around quickly. This action led Kamen to develop the self-balancing technology of the IBOT™, which uses sensors and microprocessors to keep its balance.

Kamen has been keeping his invention secret for some time, but now the news is out, and the device will become available in the not-too-distant future.

Grammar focus

1 Look at the examples. Which ones are the present perfect and which are the present perfect continuous? Label the sentences *pp* or *ppc*.

> Dean Kamen **has come up with** a design for a revolutionary new wheelchair.
> He **has been working on** projects to make people's lives better.
> Trevor Baylis **has won** several prizes for his work.
> He**'s been developing** a power device that creates electricity as people walk.

2 Look at the examples again. Complete the rules in the chart with *present perfect* or *present perfect continuous*.

Present perfect and present perfect continuous
Use the _____ to talk about past achievements. It focuses on the result of a completed action.
Use the _____ to talk about an activity that began in the past and may continue up to the present. It focuses on the continuation of an action.
To form the _____, use *have/has* + the past participle.
To form the _____, use *have/has* + *been* + *verb* + *-ing*.

Grammar Reference page 143

3 Underline the correct phrase to complete each sentence.

1. They have **built / been building** a new boat for the past year. It should be ready soon.

2. I haven't **studied / been studying** for my exam yet, and now it's too late.

3. Joanna has **won / been winning** three prizes for her paintings.

4. I've **passed / been passing** all my exams, and now I'm taking a vacation!

5. They're exhausted because they've **prepared / been preparing** for next week's sales meeting.

6. Mike has **received / been receiving** his certificate in teaching.

7. At last, she's **finished / been finishing** her chemistry project.

8. I've **read / been reading** this fascinating book about inventors. I can lend it to you when I'm done.

Pronunciation

4 🎧 **Listen. Notice the pronunciation of the weak and contracted forms of *have* and *has*.**

Trevor has won several prizes.

What else has he invented?

What have you been working on?

He's developed many windup devices.

He's been working on a device that creates electricity.

I've been developing a new computer game.

5 🎧 **Listen again and repeat.**

Speaking

6 *BEFORE YOU SPEAK.* **Write three things that you have achieved in your life and three recent ongoing activities.**

Achievements	Ongoing activities
I've received an important award at work.	I've been taking karate lessons.

7 *PAIRS.* **Talk about your achievements and ongoing activities. Ask each other follow-up questions.**

A: Barbara, tell me about something you've achieved.
B: I've received an important award at work.
A: What was it for?

8 **Tell the class about your partner's achievements and ongoing activities.**

Writing

9 **Write a brief application letter for one of the following. Include a description of your achievements and any ongoing activities.**

- an advertised job you're interested in
- a club you would like to join
- a college or university you would like to attend

CONVERSATION TO GO

A: What have you been doing lately?
B: I've been developing a new computer game. It's really cool!

29

Corporate spying

Vocabulary Crime
Grammar Expressions of purpose: *to, in order to, so that, for, in case*
Speaking Describing reasons for doing things

Getting started

1 **Underline the correct words to complete the sentences.**

1. The security guard spent the night <u>looking at</u> / **spying on** the closed circuit TVs.

2. The director **committed / was accused of** using company profits to buy a new home. He claimed he was innocent.

3. Detectives often try to **uncover / protect** people's illegal activities.

4. An employee was **suspected of / convicted of** stealing property, but it was impossible to prove.

5. When you apply for a credit card, the financial institution **restricts / checks on** your personal finances.

6. Would you please **keep an eye on / keep tabs on** my bike while I get coffee?

7. Dishonest people try to **take advantage of / get away with** cheating innocent victims.

8. Security cameras are believed to **deter / eavesdrop on** criminals.

2 *PAIRS.* **Make sentences with an appropriate form of the words you did not underline in Exercise 1.**

The police spied on the suspect for months before they arrested him.

3 *PAIRS.* **Do you think it is OK for employees to do these things at work?**

• take pens home
• send personal emails
• make personal phone calls
• claim more money on their expense accounts than they have really spent

Listening

4 🎧 **A business executive is meeting with a sales representative from a security firm. Listen to their conversation and check (✓) the picture(s) of the item or items that the executive might be interested in buying.**

5 *GROUPS OF 4.* **What is your opinion of corporate spying? Do companies have a right to spy on their workers? What rights do employees have?**

A: I think companies have to watch their workers closely in order to protect their property.
B: I think employees have a greater right to privacy.

Reading

6 Look at the photo in the magazine article. What are the security guards doing? What do you think they are looking for?

7 Read the article quickly and match the headings with the correct paragraphs.

They Know Where You Are!

Do You Take Office Pens?

Your Computer Can't Hide.

Someone's Watching You!

1.

Admit it! Sometimes you make a few personal phone calls at work. You take home some office pens. You come back a little late after lunch. You always thought nobody noticed. No one could accuse you of stealing! But not any more! From now on, employers will be taking advantage of new technology in order to spy on employees. And that means you!

2.

You may not see them, but tiny tape recorders and video cameras are probably spying on you now. They are security devices for watching and listening to everything that happens at the workplace. And don't try to hide! They can even check on workers to see if they are really where they say they are. Companies can link cameras to offices in case workers are tempted to steal property. They can install machines in sales representatives' cars to check on their expense accounts.

3.

And what's more, businesses are bringing in security companies to watch employees' virtual movements. Software is installed so that they can record the websites you visit and check the emails you send. They uncover all your secrets. You have been warned!

8 Read the article again. Write *T* (true) or *F* (false) next to each statement.

1. Companies install video cameras and tape recorders in the workplace to check that employees aren't doing anything illegal.

2. Employers put machines in their employees' cars in order to prevent the cars from being stolen.

3. "Virtual movements" in paragraph 3 refers to things people do with their computers, such as visiting websites.

4. Computer software allows employers to keep an eye on their employees' email.

Grammar focus

1 **Study the examples of expressions of purpose. Notice the ways to express reasons.**

Companies use surveillance	**to** watch employees' virtual movements.
	in order to spy on employees.
	so that they can record the websites workers visit.
	in case workers are tempted to steal property.
	for watching and listening to everything.

2 **Look at the examples again. Complete the rules in the chart with *verb*, *verb + -ing*, or *subject + verb*.**

Expressions of purpose

Why someone does something:	Because something might happen:
to + ___verb___	in case + _____
in order to + _____	**What something is for:**
so that + _____	for + _____

> Grammar Reference page 143

3 **Use *to, in order to, so that, in case,* and *for*. Combine the beginnings of the sentences on the left with the endings on the right to make logical sentences.**

Some companies use microphones and video cameras to find evidence of dishonest employees.

1. Some companies use microphones and video cameras

2. Cell phones are very useful

3. Before you start a trip, you should leave all your contact information with a relative

4. Security cameras are used in stores

5. Many people use identification devices in their phones

6. Some companies use software

7. Some parents install hidden video cameras at home

8. The police sometimes use hidden microphones

a. there is an emergency.

b. catching shoplifters.

c. watching the babysitter while they're out.

d. they can ignore unwanted calls.

e. they can check on employees' computer use.

f. find evidence of dishonest employees.

g. eavesdrop on criminals.

h. staying in contact with teenagers while they're out with friends.

Pronunciation

4 *PAIRS.* One word in each line does not have the stress shown by the pattern of big and small circles. Underline the word that has a different stress pattern.

⬤ ○	problems, cameras, suspect (noun), <u>protect</u>, software
○ ⬤	deter, office, suspect (verb), accused, install
⬤ ○ ○	company, evidence, monitor, criminal, surveillance
○ ⬤ ○	property, solutions, employees, advantage, devices
○ ⬤ ○ ○	security, technology, information, responsible

5 🎧 Listen and check your answers. Notice the stress in the words.

6 🎧 Listen again and repeat.

Speaking

7 *PAIRS.* Imagine you have the following jobs. You and your partner are going to have a meeting about company security.

Student A, look at page 137. Student B, look at page 141.

A: *Our employees may be making long personal calls because our phone bill went up by 30 percent. Can you help me with this problem?*
B: *Yes, we can. We have something called "Call Stopper," which many companies use to stop long phone calls.*
A: *How much does it cost?*

8 Report to the class what you and your partner agreed on and the reasons for the decision.

Writing

9 You are the president of a company. Write an email to your employees. Explain some new security devices that you are going to start using or stop using. Explain the reason for your decision.

CONVERSATION TO GO

A: Why are you putting in security cameras?
B: **So that** I'll know where I am.

33

Up in the air

Vocabulary   Travel and airports
Grammar   Past perfect
Speaking   Talking about events in your life

Getting started

1 *PAIRS.* **Look at the pictures of people, places, and things related to air travel. Write the letters of the pictures next to the correct words.**

baggage claim _G_	luggage ____
boarding pass ____	flight attendant ____
carry-on bag ____	gate ____
check-in counter ____	runway ____
duty-free shops ____	security checkpoint ____

2 *PAIRS.* **Take turns asking each other these questions. Explain what happened and ask and answer follow-up questions.**

Have you ever . . .
• missed a flight?
• lost your luggage?
• gone to the wrong gate?
• been stopped at a security checkpoint?
• had any other problems while traveling?

Reading ◀━━━━━

3 Read the article quickly. Did the traveler have a positive or negative experience at the airport?

LOSING YOURSELF AT THE AIRPORT

The Hub

Sometimes you fly, not to your destination, but to a "hub." In other words, you have to change planes at some airport you never cared to be in. You sit in the airport lounge where all the seats face the same direction, like the seats in a theater, with nothing to do but kill time.

You drift off to sleep. When you wake up, you don't know what time it is. In many airports, each terminal is the same as every other terminal. The corridors are also all the same. But gate 36 may be hundreds of meters from gate 35, in any direction—it's easy to make a mistake.

I was once at an airport in Zurich. The weather was bad and the plane was delayed. I went to a café. I sat there drinking coffee and reading a book. Outside, the weather had gotten worse. Time passed. When the flight was announced, I picked up my bags and moved toward the gate. I went down a corridor, down some steps, straight for a bit, down for a bit. Then, just as I got to the gate, I realized I had left my book in the café.

I tried to remember the route I had taken so I could do it in reverse. I was successful. The book was still there. Then I started running back. I ran up staircases, along corridors. At some point, I knew that I had taken the wrong turn. I panicked.

Adapted from *The Observer* newspaper

4 Read the article again. Write *T* (true) or *F* (false) after each statement.

1. You land at a hub to catch another plane.
2. It is easy to go to the wrong gate.
3. When the author went back, he couldn't find the book.
4. The author got lost in the airport.

Listening ◀━━━━━

5 🎧 Listen to two people talking at an airport while they wait for their plane. What happened to Lou? Number the events in the correct order.

_1_ He got delayed in traffic.   ___ The plane returned to the gate.

___ He boarded the plane.   ___ He was late for his flight.

___ The plane left the gate.   ___ He went to the gate.

6 *PAIRS.* **Was Lou right to do what he did? Would you do the same thing?**

8

Grammar focus

1 **Study the example of the past perfect. Notice the timeline.**

By the time he reached the gate, his plane **had** already **left**.

the plane left   now

he reached the gate

2 **Look at the examples again. Underline the correct information to complete the rules in the chart.**

Past perfect
Use the past perfect to talk about an action that happened **before / after** another action in the past.
Form the past perfect with *had* + the **infinitive / past participle**.
When you use *already* with the past perfect, it goes **before / after** *had*.
Use the **simple past / past perfect** tense in clauses that begin with *by the time*.
NOTE: You can use contractions with subject pronouns and *had*; for example, **He'd** *gotten stuck*.

Grammar Reference page 144

3 **Complete the sentences using the correct form of the past perfect or the simple past of the verbs in parentheses.**

1. He _got_____ (**get**) to the airport late because he _had gotten stuck_____ (**get stuck**) in traffic.

2. When we got to the beach, we _____ (**want**) to go swimming, but we realized that we _____ (**not/pack**) our swimsuits.

3. We _____ (**have**) a wonderful time on our skiing vacation. The kids _____ (**never/see**) snow before.

4. As soon as I saw Jong-Mi, I _____ (**realize**) I _____ (**meet**) her before.

5. I knew I _____ (**not/study**) enough as soon as I _____ (**see**) the first exam question.

6. I _____ (**not/laugh**) at the joke because I _____ (**hear**) it so many times before.

7. When she _____ (**ask**) to see my boarding pass, I realized I _____ (**lose**) it.

8. I _____ (**not/call**) you this morning because I thought you _____ (**already/go out**).

Pronunciation

4 🎧 **Listen. Notice the pronunciation of the weak and contracted forms of *had*.**

I'd forgotten my book.

He'd already checked out of the hotel.

His plane ~had~ already left the gate.

I realized I ~had~ left it in the café.

He was late because he'd gotten stuck in traffic.

But it **hadn't** taken off yet.

5 🎧 **Listen again and repeat.**

Speaking

6 *BEFORE YOU SPEAK.* **Think of something interesting or important that happened to you. It could be about travel, your family, your job, or something else.**

- Decide on six key words or events in the story.
- Write them in the boxes in the order they happened.

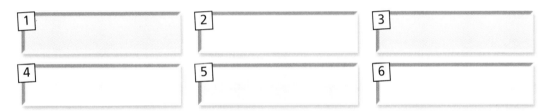

7 *PAIRS.* **Tell the story of your experience. Start at number four (in the past). For things that happened before then, use the past perfect.**

I missed a plane. I'd been on vacation and had already checked out of the hotel. I was late because I'd gotten stuck in traffic on the way to the airport.

Writing

8 **Write a story of an interesting experience that happened to you or to someone you know. Use the past perfect tense.**

CONVERSATION TO GO

A: Did you say good-bye to her at the airport?
B: No. By the time I arrived, her flight **had** already **left**.

Unit 5 How rude!

1 *PAIRS.* Role-play the following situations. Take turns asking for and giving/denying permission.

1. Your neighbor has no hot water in her home. She knocks at your door and asks you if she can use your bathroom.

2. You are sitting at an outdoor café when a man at the next table wants to smoke. You can't stand smoke anywhere near you.

3. A friend who is staying with you wants to use your phone to call his or her brother in England.

4. You are the boss at work. Someone who works for you needs to leave early today. This person has arrived late every day this week.

5. You are in a waiting room in a doctor's office with a few other people. There's a TV that's not turned on. Another person wants to turn on the TV.

2 Create two new situations and role-play them.

Unit 6 Achievement

3 🎧 Listen to a description of an achievement by an inventor. Answer these questions.

1. What has Mohammed Bah Abba invented?

2. What does his invention do?

3. What has he been trying to do since he came up with his idea?

4 *GROUPS OF 3.* Can you think of any inventions or achievements that have changed the way we live, in small or big ways? Describe them and explain how they have made a difference.

Mohammed Bah Abba

5 Read the article about camera phones. What are the arguments for and against their use?

In the Public Eye

One evening last month, grocery store owner Sam Lee was about to close his shop when a man came in, waving a knife at Sam and demanding money. Instead of giving him money, Sam pulled out his cell phone and used it to snap a picture of the robber. The man ran off, but within minutes, Sam had transmitted the picture to his computer. When police arrived, Sam had the man's picture waiting for them.

Camera phones may be used for spying on people who don't suspect it. For example, police could use camera phones in order to identify criminals or missing persons, but they could also use them to photograph protestors. Some fitness centers have banned camera phones so that they can keep spying eyes out of locker rooms. Businesses are already looking into ways of using camera phones in order to check on employees' whereabouts. Critics worry that these phones may change our way of life, and not for the better.

6 *PAIRS.* Have a debate for and against the use of camera phones. Give examples of what people will use them for.

Unit 8 Up in the air

7 🎧 *PAIRS.* Listen to a conversation between two friends. Complete the story with your own ideas.

8 *PAIRS.* Take turns telling stories of interesting travel experiences that happened to you or someone you know. Give the background details of what had happened earlier.

UNIT
9

Sunshine and showers

Vocabulary The weather
Grammar Indirect statements
Speaking Reporting what you hear or read

Lesson A

A

B

C

Getting started

1 Complete the sentences with the words in the box. There may be more than one answer.

~~cloud cover~~	clouds	fog	rain
showers	snow	sunshine	thunderstorms
tornado	winds		

1. It isn't raining today, but there is a very thick _cloud cover_ .

2. There was heavy _____ during the night and some roads were flooded.

3. You probably won't need an umbrella—there will be just light _____ today.

4. A tree was hit by lightning during severe _____ yesterday.

5. During the summer in Greece, there is bright _____ every day.

6. _____ will fall tonight, especially in the mountains.

7. There were very strong _____, and several trees were blown down.

8. It was difficult to see while I was driving because of the dense _____.

9. A deadly _____ carved its path across the region.

10. Look at those dark _____! It's going to rain any minute.

2 *PAIRS.* Discuss these questions.

What kind of weather is typical of different parts of your country?
Are there any sayings (or proverbs) about the weather in your country?

40

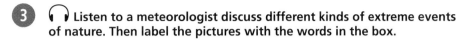

Listening

3 🎧 Listen to a meteorologist discuss different kinds of extreme events of nature. Then label the pictures with the words in the box.

| hurricane / typhoon   tornado   tsunami |

Reading

4 *PAIRS.* Look at the photo in the newspaper article. What do you think happened?

5 Read the newspaper article and answer these questions.

1. When do tornados often happen?

2. What was the main cause of this unusual tornado?

3. What were three results of the tornado?

4. What other word for *tornado* can you find in the article?

6 *PAIRS.* Discuss. What extreme events from nature do you fear most? Why?

November 13   *The Times*

A Twist of Fate
Deadly Tornado Hits Small Town

Birch Grove, November 13 — It was nice and calm at noon yesterday, though unusually hot for November. In the evening, dark clouds appeared, then lightning and rain started, and then came the wind. Suddenly, a devastating tornado swept across the region, leaving at least five people dead and others missing.

Speaking at a press conference late last night, the Governor said that thousands of people in neighboring towns were without electricity, but that the lights would be back on by tonight.

The twister left a deadly path behind it. Meteorologist Mark Chaves, describing the devastation, said, "I saw mobile homes thrown into ponds and entire forests wiped out." Tornadoes are common in the spring,

The Farkas family surveys the damage to their home.

rare in the fall. But Chaves said that unseasonably warm weather had made all the difference.

Harry Coleman, a resident from the area, was out of town when he got a call from his wife on his cell phone.

She told him that their son and grandson were missing. Other residents were luckier. John and Rebecca Reilly's home lost electricity in the rainstorm, but no one was harmed.

Police officer Al Barton said, "I heard a roar and saw the lightning just before the twister came. Then I watched the twister pick up houses and cars, and toss them like toys." Police and rescue crews are still searching for the missing, but dense fog is making their job all the more difficult.

Only a few houses in Birch Grove have basements, and Susan Farkas and her family took shelter in theirs. Within minutes, the house above them began to peel away. Daughter Ginny said, "We all held on to each other and somehow we survived." As the Farkases looked over their broken furniture lying on the ground, Susan told her daughter, "I can't believe it. Yesterday we had a nice house, and today we don't even have a toothbrush."

Grammar focus

1 **Study the examples. Notice the differences between direct and indirect statements.**

Direct statements	Indirect statements
"Our son and grandson are missing."	She **told him (that) their** son and grandson **were** missing.
"I can't believe it."	Susan **said (that)** she **couldn't** believe it.
"The lights will be on by tomorrow night."	Last night the governor **said (that)** the lights **would be** on by **tonight**.
"Unseasonably warm weather made all the difference."	Chaves **said (that)** unseasonably warm weather **had made** all the difference.

2 **Look at the examples again. Complete the rules in the chart with *change* or *don't change*.**

Indirect statements
When changing from direct statements to indirect statements using *said* or *told* + object:
The tenses usually _____.
The time expressions usually _____.
The possessive adjectives and pronouns usually _____.
NOTE: The word *that* is optional after *say* or *tell*.

Grammar Reference page 144

3 **Rewrite the sentences in indirect speech. Make any necessary changes.**

1. He said, "Thousands of people are still without electricity."

   He said that thousands of people were still without electricity.

2. They said, "It is one of the worst tornadoes in years."

3. He said, "I saw mobile homes thrown into ponds."

4. Susan told her daughter, "We don't even have a toothbrush."

5. He said, "I heard a roar and saw the lightning."

6. She told me, "Somehow we survived."

7. The Governor said, "The government will do everything it can to assist families."

8. Last night the meteorologist said, "It's unlikely there will be any more tornadoes tonight."

Pronunciation

4 🎧 **Listen. Notice the pronunciation of the voiceless *th* sound /θ/ in the words in the first row and the voiced *th* sound /ð/ in the words in the second row.**

thunderstorm	**th**ousands	every**th**ing	**th**rown	pa**th**
they	**th**ere	wi**th**out	o**th**er	**th**e wea**th**er

What did **th**ey say about **th**e wea**th**er?   **Th**ey said **th**ere would be **th**ick clouds and **th**understorms.

5 🎧 **Listen again and repeat.**

Speaking

6 *GROUPS OF 3.* **You've made plans to have a beach party tomorrow. You're each getting the weather forecast from a different TV channel. Based on the weather forecasts, decide together if you are still going to the beach.**

Student A, look at page 137. Student B, look at page 138. Student C, look at page 140.

On Channel 12 they said that there was a storm coming from the south. It will probably rain at times.

7 **Look at page 141 to check the actual weather on the day of the beach party. Was your decision correct?**

Writing

8 **Write an email to a friend who is planning to visit you tomorrow. Tell your friend how the weather is today and what you think it will be like tomorrow.**

CONVERSATION TO GO

A: Have you heard the weather report?
B: Yes. They said there would be heavy rain all day.

UNIT 10

Tomorrow's world

Vocabulary	Describing changes
Grammar	Simple future and future perfect
Speaking	Predicting future events

Lesson A

Getting started

1 *PAIRS.* **Look at the pairs of words. Underline the three additional pairs that describe up/down changes.**

<u>go up / go down</u>	decrease / increase	fall / rise
improve / deteriorate	climb / drop	get better / get worse

2 *PAIRS.* **Look at the list of topics. Make predictions about them. Use the words from Exercise 1 in your predictions.**

I think pollution will start to decrease.

- pollution
- crime
- health care
- life expectancy
- quality of life
- education

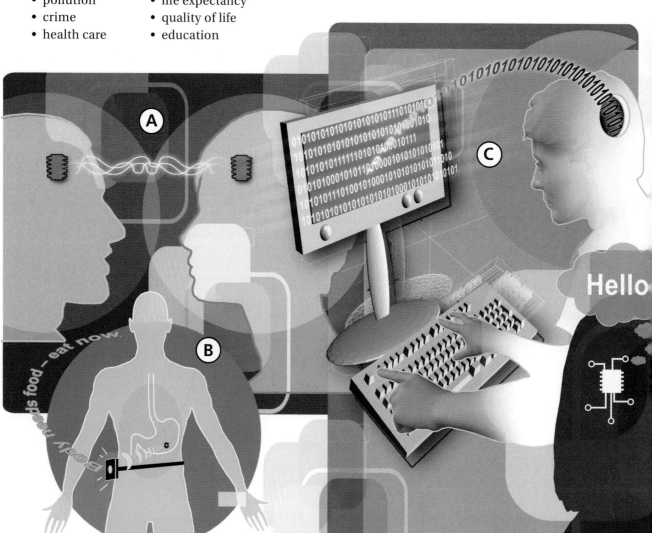

44

Reading

3 Look at the pictures of future technological advances and describe what you think is happening in each.

It looks like computers inside the people's brains are communicating with each other.

4 Read the magazine article about predictions for technological advances. Write the letter of each picture next to the paragraph that describes it.

What Will the Future Look Like?

A bright future or Frankenstein's monster?

_____ By 2075, scientists will have produced edible computers—you can eat one per day. They will record everything that's going on inside you and carry this information to a small box that you wear on your belt. These systems will be invaluable to doctors and will dramatically improve health care.

_____ Methods of communication are advancing—by the year 2150, scientists will have perfected the "brainlink" computer. A tiny computer will be implanted under the skin on the back of people's heads, which will tell their brains how to speak any language they need. Just imagine! People will be able to go to another country and order a meal in a restaurant without using a dictionary!

_____ Computers could be connected to people's brains by the end of the 22nd century. As a result, the number of schools will decrease, or they may even disappear completely. People will simply be able to download information into their heads. Imagine being able to store all the knowledge you need in your brain without memorizing!

_____ By the 23rd century, scientists will have developed a technique for implanting computer chips in people's brains. People will be able to communicate by simply using their brainwaves. But will they want to?

5 Read the article again. What do you think will be the benefit of each technological advance?

- edible computers
- "brainlink" computers
- computers connected to brains
- implanted computer chips

Listening

6 🎧 Listen to the radio interview with Dr. Pierce. Write a plus sign (+) next to the technological advances in Exercise 5 that she thinks are positive, and a minus sign (–) next to the ones she thinks are negative.

7 *PAIRS.* Discuss these questions.

Do you think these advances will actually happen?

If they do, do you think they will improve or worsen people's lives? Why?

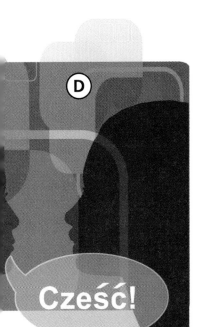

(D)

Cześć!

Grammar focus

1 **Study the examples. Notice the difference between the sentences in the simple future and those in the future perfect tense.**

Simple future	Future perfect
We**'ll be** able to swallow tiny computers.	By the year 2150, scientists **will have perfected** the "brainlink" computer.
They**'ll record** everything that's going on.	By 2075, they**'ll have produced** edible computers.

2 **Look at the examples again. Underline the correct words to complete the rules in the chart.**

Simple future and future perfect

Form the simple future with **will / will have** + the base form of the verb.

Form the future perfect with **will / will have** + past participle.

Use the simple future when you expect something to happen **at / before** some point in the future.

Use the future perfect when you expect something to happen **at / before** some point in the future.

> *Grammar Reference page 144*

3 **Use the cues to complete the sentences. Use only one word in each blank.**

1. Life expectancy will have _____increased_____ (**increase**) to over 100 by 2070.

2. Someday all cars will _____ (**use**) energy from the sun instead of gas.

3. In the next five years, communication will _____ (**become**) much quicker.

4. Within 50 years, they will have _____ (**invent**) cars that reach a destination by themselves.

5. In the next 100 years there will _____ (**be**) cures for every known disease.

6. By the end of this century, they will have _____ (**build**) underground cities in many countries around the world.

7. Someday blind people will _____ (**have**) robots to guide them.

8. By 2025, keys will have _____ (**disappear**). Instead, special sensors will _____ (**identify**) people and open doors for them.

4 **PAIRS. Which predictions in Exercise 3 do you agree with? Explain.**

Pronunciation

5 🎧 **Listen. Notice the pronunciation of the contracted and weak forms of *will* and the way *will* is linked to the weak form of *have*.**

We'll be able to swallow tiny computers.

Communication will be easier.

We'll ḥave learned to communicate by brainwaves.

They'll record what's going on.

Scientists will ḥave perfected the brainlink computer.

They'll ḥave found ways to read people's thoughts.

6 🎧 **Listen again and repeat.**

Speaking

7 *BEFORE YOU SPEAK.* **Think about your future. Where will you be and what will you have accomplished? Think about at least three ideas related to things like education, career, family, sports, hobbies and travel. Take notes.**

8 *PAIRS.* **Take turns talking about your predictions for the future.**

I predict that by the year 2010, I will have bought a house.

9 **Report to the class. What were at least two predictions your partner made?**

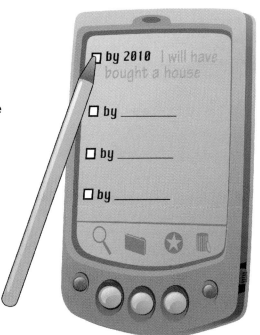

☐ by 2010 I will have bought a house
☐ by _____
☐ by _____
☐ by _____

Writing

10 **Write a diary entry about things you believe you will have done five years from now. Write about career, marriage, family, travel, or any other things you can imagine will have happened.**

CONVERSATION TO GO

A: When will you be finished with your homework? Dinner will be ready in about an hour.

B: I'll probably have finished it by breakfast time tomorrow!

How did it go?

Vocabulary   Job interviews
Grammar   Indirect questions
Speaking   Reporting a conversation or interview

Lesson A

I really hope I get the job.

Getting started

1 *PAIRS.* **Discuss these questions.**

Which kinds of interviews have you been on?
How do you feel before, during, and after an interview?

2 *PAIRS.* **Look at the "Top Tips for Job Interviews" and underline the correct word or phrase in each tip.**

Top Tips for Job Interviews

1 Make a list of your **strengths / prospects**.
It's important to talk about what you are good at.

2 Make a list of your **qualifications / weaknesses**. Interviewers sometimes ask what you are *not* good at.

3 Prepare to talk about your past **experience / promotion**. You can talk about things you have done that relate to this job.

4 Make sure you know which relevant **qualifications / long-term goals** you have. Certificates, diplomas, and degrees are important.

5 Think of two past employers who will write good **prospects / references** for you. The interviewer will need to know what past employers thought of your work.

6 Show that you are interested in **experience / promotion**. It's impressive to show interest in getting better jobs in the company in the future.

7 Be clear about your **long-term goals / qualifications**. Interviewers sometimes ask what your five-year plan is.

8 Be realistic about your job **references / prospects**. Don't waste your time applying for a job if you know you are unqualified.

Reading

3 *PAIRS.* **Read the list of tips in Exercise 2 again. Match each of these statements with the correct tip.**

1. "I have a degree in communications."
2. "I think I work well under pressure, and I'm well organized."
3. "I used to work at a bank. My former supervisor would be glad to recommend me."
4. "Because I like to work fast, I sometimes do things in a bit of a hurry."
5. "I'd like to move from sales to management someday."
6. "I was treasurer of my school's computer club, so I'm used to handling money."

4 *GROUPS OF 3.* **Discuss the following as they apply to your school or work life.**

My main strength is creativity, I think. I find it fun to work with new ideas.

- your main strengths
- your qualifications
- your long-term goals

So, how did it go?

That's great news!

Listening

5 🎧 **Listen to Carol telling a friend about her job interview. Check (✓) the topics discussed in the interview.**

- ☐ previous experience
- ☐ working under pressure
- ☐ strengths
- ☐ long-term goals
- ☐ weaknesses
- ☐ reasons for leaving previous jobs
- ☐ salary
- ☐ taking breaks during work

6 🎧 **Listen again and answer these questions.**

1. How does Carol think the interview went?
2. What did she ask the interviewer about?
3. Did the interview go better or worse than Carol thought? How do you know?

Grammar focus

1 **Study the examples. Notice the differences between direct and indirect questions.**

Direct questions	Indirect questions
A. "What are your strengths?"	She asked me **what my strengths were**.
B. "Do you have other weaknesses?"	She wanted me to tell her **if I had other weaknesses**.
C. "Can you work under pressure?"	She wanted to know **whether I could work under pressure**.

2 **Look at the examples again. Underline the correct words to complete the rules in the chart.**

Indirect questions
The verb tense in direct and indirect questions is often the **same / different**.
For indirect questions that ask for information (example A), use **a Wh- word / if**.
For indirect *Yes/No* questions (examples B and C), use **a Wh- word / if**.
In indirect questions, use **subject + verb / verb + subject** after the *Wh-* word or *if*.
NOTE: With indirect questions, *if* and *whether* mean the same thing.

Grammar Reference page 144

3 **Change the direct questions to indirect questions. Use different ways of starting indirect questions.**

He wanted to know what the responsibilities of the job were. OR
He asked her what the responsibilities of the job were.

1. What are the responsibilities of the job?
2. How did you hear about our company?
3. What qualifications do I need for the job?
4. Where have you worked before?
5. Do I have to wear a uniform?
6. How long did you stay at your last job?
7. What type of work will be involved?
8. Do you speak any foreign languages?
9. Who will I work with?
10. Can you work some weekends?

Pronunciation

4 🎧 **Listen. Notice the groups of consonant sounds in these words.**

pressure	**pr**omotion	**pr**o**sp**e**cts**	e**xp**erie**nc**e
stay	**st**art	**str**e**ngths**	a**sked**

She a**sked** about my **pr**evious e**xp**erie**nc**e. She a**sked** me what my **str**e**ngths** were.

I to**ld** her I work well under **pr**essure. I a**sked** her about the **pr**o**sp**e**cts** for **pr**omotion.

She a**sked** me how long I **pl**anned to **st**ay. She a**sked** me when I could **st**art.

5 🎧 **Listen again and repeat.**

Speaking

6 *BEFORE YOU SPEAK.* **Think about a situation when someone asked you questions. The situation might be a job interview, a first date, a visit to the doctor, etc. Complete the chart.**

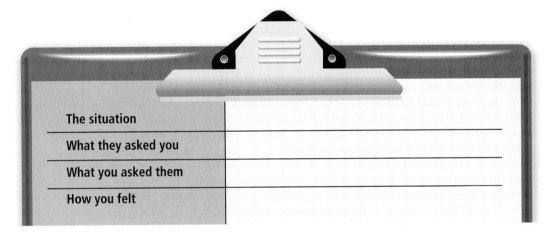

The situation	
What they asked you	
What you asked them	
How you felt	

7 *PAIRS.* **Take turns describing the situation.**

I had an interview for a part-time job when I was in high school. They asked me why I was interested . . .

Writing

8 **Write a letter to a friend describing an interview or a conversation with someone who asked you questions. Explain the situation, and then report the questions and the answers.**

CONVERSATION TO GO

A: How did it go?
B: Great! He **asked me if I wanted** the job.

Lesson A

Coincidences

Vocabulary Time adverbials
Grammar Narrative past tenses: simple past, past continuous, past perfect, past perfect continuous
Speaking Telling stories in the past

Getting started

1 *PAIRS.* **Choose two words or phrases from the box that can replace each word or phrase in bold.**

afterward	at the same time
earlier	every time
previously	simultaneously
subsequently	whenever

1. Have you ever been introduced to someone but forgotten their name **later**?

   afterward / subsequently

2. Are there any places that remind you of someone **each time** you go there?

   _____ / _____

3. Have you ever experienced something that you had dreamed about **before**?

   _____ / _____

4. Have you and another person ever said exactly the same thing **at the same moment**?

   _____ / _____

2 *PAIRS.* **Take turns asking and answering the questions in Exercise 1.**

Reading

3 Look at the pictures in the article. What do you think is happening in each?

4 Read about some real-life coincidences. Then match the titles with the stories.

Family Reunion

The Wrong Number

A Shared History

Life Saver

5   Read the article again. Explain in your own words what each coincidence was.

6   *PAIRS.* **Discuss these questions.**

Which coincidence do you find most amazing?

Which would you describe as a lucky coincidence? A strange coincidence?

You'll Never Believe It!

1. _____

John Peskett—who first met his wife, Shirley, when he was 21—discovered, when she showed him her favorite childhood photo, that he and his family had been sitting next to her on the same beach twenty years earlier.

2. _____

A young man, Harold Archer, threw himself in front of a train, but was saved—an inch from death—by a passenger on the train who had pulled the emergency cord without knowing about Archer. The passenger said afterward that she had pulled the cord because she "suddenly felt she should."

3. _____

Charlie Crook one day decided to drive over 100 miles (160 km) to visit his cousin, John Barker, whom he hadn't seen for eight years. Barker had simultaneously decided to drive and see Charlie—and met him halfway, where their cars collided.

4. _____

Police officer Peter Moscardi, on night patrol, became suspicious when he saw an open door in a factory. He entered the factory office and decided to pick up a phone that was ringing. It was a friend of his calling to chat. Moscardi had previously given his friend the police station phone's last four numbers incorrectly—that number was the factory's telephone number.

Adapted from ES Magazine

Listening

7   Listen to a man tell the story of an event that happened to him. Answer these questions.

1. What was the coincidence?
2. How do you think the man felt when he realized what had happened?

Grammar focus

1 **Study the examples of narrative past tenses. Notice how different tenses are used.**

> A passenger on the train **pulled** the emergency cord.
>
> He **decided** to pick up a phone that **was ringing**.
>
> He **discovered** that he and his family **had been sitting** next to her on the same beach twenty years earlier.
>
> Charlie Crook **decided** to visit his cousin, John Barker, whom he **hadn't seen** for eight years.

2 **Look at the examples again. Complete the rules in the chart with *simple past*, *past continuous*, *past perfect*, or *past perfect continuous*.**

Narrative past tenses: simple past, past continuous, past perfect, past perfect continuous
_____ refers to an action that was in progress when something else happened.
_____ refers to a completed action in the past.
_____ refers to an action completed before another event or time in the past.
_____ refers to an action that was in progress before another event or time in the past.

Grammar Reference page 145

3 **Read the story. Then put the verbs into the correct tenses.**

Irene Jones and Stella Frank, both from Texas, ___grew up___
1. (grow up)

on the same street and _____ best friends. Stella was
2. (become)

Irene's bridesmaid at her wedding. Then Irene moved away,

and they _____ touch. Fifty-three years later,
3. (lose)

they _____ into each other while they
4. (bump)

_____ in line at a gas station in Boulder,
5. (wait)

Colorado. They immediately _____ each
6. (recognize)

other, even though they _____ each other
7. (not see)

for over fifty years. While they _____ ,
8. (talk)

they _____ they _____ in the same
9. (find out)   10. (live)

neighborhood in Boulder for 17 years, but _____
11. (never see)

each other until that day.

54

Pronunciation

4 🎧 Listen to the beginning of the story in Exercise 3. Notice that only the important words are stressed.

Irene Jones and **Stella Frank**, **both** from **Tex**as, grew **up** on the **same street**.

5 🎧 Listen to more of the story. Underline the stressed words on page 54.

Speaking

6 *BEFORE YOU SPEAK.* What are five important events in your life (for example, you got your first job, you graduated from school, you got married, etc.)? Think about the events that led up to each one. Take notes.

Date, important event	Background
2000: I graduated from school	I had been studying for four years and . . .

7 *GROUPS OF 4.* Take turns talking about the special events in your life and the events that led up to them.

8 Report to the class. Are there any coincidences or similarities between the events in your group?

Two years ago, I moved to this area. I had been living in Pleasantville before. It turns out that Marta had once lived in Pleasantville, too.

Writing

9 Write a story about several important events in your life and the circumstances that led up to them.

CONVERSATION TO GO

A: What were you doing at ten o'clock last night, sir?
B: I was watching TV. I'd been out with my friends in the afternoon.

Unit 9 Sunshine and showers

1 🎧 *GROUPS OF 4.* Listen to weather forecasts for different cities. Each student listens to the report for one city and takes notes.

Student	City	Today	Tomorrow
A	Tokyo, Japan		
B	Ottawa, Canada		
C	Recife, Brazil		
D	Santiago, Chile		

2 *GROUPS OF 4.* Take turns reporting on the forecasts you took notes on. What did the meteorologist say about the weather now and for the future? Take notes on your partners' reports.

Unit 10 Tomorrow's world

3 🎧 Listen to a conversation between two friends about a movie called *Sleeper*. What is the movie about?

4 Imagine you fall asleep and wake up 200 years in the future. Write down some ideas about what will have happened by the time you wake up, and how life will be different in the 23rd century.

5 *PAIRS.* Discuss your ideas about the future.

Unit 11 How did it go?

6 Read the ad. You are going to role-play an interview for the job advertised.

> ## Salesperson Wanted
>
> Excellent opportunity to be a salesperson in an electronics superstore. Competitive salary & benefits. Experience in sales and/or electronics is preferred. Work some nights/weekends. Call 555-4321.

7 *PAIRS.* Role-play the job interview.

Student A, look at page 139. Student B, look at page 140.

8 *GROUPS OF 4.* Report the questions and answers from your interview in Exercise 7.

A: I asked him if he had any sales experience.
C: And what did he say?

Unit 12 Coincidences

9 Read the facts in "All in the family" related to the story of three men. What was their relationship? Why was it an amazing coincidence?

10 *PAIRS.* Together, tell the story of Gary and his long-lost brothers. You can start like this:

When Gary's first child was born, his parents told him that he was an adopted child. That conversation changed his life forever.

11 *PAIRS.* Do you know any stories of amazing coincidences? Take turns telling the stories. Include any background information.

All in the family

- Steve and Gary were best friends. In fact, they were like brothers; Gary was best man at Steve's wedding.

- Steve was adopted. He knew this but didn't know his real parents.

- Gary was adopted too, but he didn't know it because his parents never told him.

- Gary had a good friend named Richard who worked out at the same fitness center.

- Richard was also adopted but didn't know who his real parents were.

- After Gary's first child was born, his parents decided to tell him that he was adopted.

- When Gary found out that he was adopted, he got together with Steve and Richard. Pretty soon, they figured out that they were all brothers! They learned later that they were among nine children given up for adoption by a couple who had thirteen children.

- The brothers were shocked, but delighted, to find each other. Gary said it was "the greatest gift in the world."

World of Music 2

Words Get in the Way
Gloria Estefan

Vocabulary

1 *PAIRS.* Match the clauses on the left with the appropriate information on the right to make logical sentences.

1. I've been **seeing** __f__

2. I never know what to expect from my best friend because ____

3. It's hard to be with someone who ____

4. When I have **something on my mind**, ____

5. Some people get very nervous if they feel ____

6. When you lose someone you love, ____

7. I don't let my social life ____

8. Animals who were born in captivity often die ____

9. If someone's heart is **an open door**, ____

10. You can still love someone ____

a. I like to talk about it.

b. **despite the fact that** he or she causes you pain.

c. is **temperamental**.

d. it's easy to know how they feel.

e. it **breaks your heart**.

f. someone new.

g. **get in the way** of work or school.

h. if you **set** them **free**.

i. he's totally **moody**. He changes from happy to mad, to happy again five times a day!

j. **locked** inside a small place, such as an elevator.

Gloria Estefan was born in Cuba in 1957. She started her musical career in 1975, when she sang at a wedding where a local band was playing. The band leader, Emilio Estefan, was so impressed by Gloria's voice that he asked her to join his band. Gloria Estefan has enjoyed many successful hits, including "Let it Loose," "Into the Light," and "Gloria!"

Listening

2 🎧 Listen to "Words Get in the Way," by Gloria Estefan. Which statement is true about the singer and her boyfriend? Circle the letter of the correct answer.

a. She doesn't know how to tell him that she doesn't love him anymore.

b. She's been trying to tell him that he's too temperamental.

c. She has strong feelings but can't express them.

3 🎧 Listen to the song again and complete the lyrics on page 59.

Words Get in the Way

I realize you're seeing someone new.

I don't believe she knows you like I do;

Your temperamental moody side,

the one you always try to hide from me.

But I know when you have something on your mind.

_____ _____ _____ to tell me for the longest time.

And before you break my heart in two,

There's something _____ _____ _____ to say to you.

But the words get in the way.

There's so much I want to say,

But it's locked deep inside, and if you _____ in
    my eyes

We _____ fall in love again.

I won't even start to cry and before we say good-bye.

I tried to say I love you,

But the words got in the way.

Your heart _____ always _____ an open door,

But baby, I don't even know you anymore.

And despite the fact it's hurting me,

I know the time _____ _____ to set you free.

But the words get in the way.

There's so much I want to say,

But it's locked deep inside and if you _____ in
    my eyes

We _____ fall in love again.

I won't even start to cry and before we say good-bye.

I tried to say I love you,

But the words got in the way.

I'm trying to say I love you,

But the words get in the way.

Speaking

4 **GROUPS OF 3.** Discuss these questions. Use lines from the song to explain your answers.

1. Has the singer's boyfriend told her that he's been dating someone else?
2. What does the singer wish for?
3. What does she want to say to her boyfriend? Why can't she say it?

5 *PAIRS.* Discuss. Have you ever experienced a time when "the words got in the way"?
Explain.

Going it alone

Vocabulary Adjectives describing fear, loneliness, and nervousness
Grammar Present unreal conditional (*If* + simple past tense form + *would* + verb)
Speaking Talking about hypothetical situations

Getting started

1 *PAIRS.* **Look at the adjectives that describe fear, loneliness, and nervousness. Write them next to the words that have similar meanings.**

~~cut off~~	fearful
jumpy	lonesome
solitary	stressed out
isolated	tense
petrified	jittery
scared	terrified

afraid

lonely

cut off

nervous

100 days at sea

At the age of 24, Ellen MacArthur became the youngest and the smallest (she is just under 5 feet 2 inches—1.57 meters) competitor to take part in the Vendée Globe race—the biggest challenge in sailing: 100 days alone at sea.

Imagine how it would feel sailing single-handed, nonstop, and unaided around the world, without seeing another person for weeks on end, without knowing when a hurricane could hit your boat and end your chances of finishing or even surviving.

To sail the roughest seas alone, you need great ability and strength —Ellen has both. She remembers everything she reads and hears. "You need so many different skills," Ellen says. "Alone at sea, you are a sailor, an electrician, an engineer, and a cook. There is so much to do so you never feel lonely. I wouldn't do it if I were scared of being alone."

In order to avoid fatigue, Ellen trained to sleep for as little as twenty minutes at a time. "Normal sleep is impossible; you can't sleep for more than four hours a day. If you needed more sleep, you could never finish the race."

During her incredible voyage, she battled against ocean storms, fatigue, and 23 much more experienced competitors, who were mostly men. By the force of her character, Ellen eventually took second place and became a legend.

2 🎧 **Listen and check your answers.**

3 *PAIRS.* **Discuss these questions.**

How do you feel about being . . .
- alone?
- in the dark?
- on an airplane?
- in a very small space?

Lesson A

Reading

4 *PAIRS.* **Look at the photo and discuss these questions.**

Where is this woman?

What is she doing?

How do you think she is feeling?

5 **Read the article to see if your ideas were correct.**

6 **Read the article again. Write *T* (true) or *F* (false) after each statement.**

1. Nobody can help the sailors during the race.
2. Ellen is afraid of being alone.
3. During the race, Ellen had little sleep.
4. Ellen was one of the most experienced competitors in the race.
5. She came in second, so she wasn't very successful.

Listening

7 🎧 **Listen to the radio show discussing Ellen MacArthur's life. Answer these questions.**

1. Is Ellen afraid of anything? If so, what?

2. Has she ever finished last in a race? When?

3. Does she think she will win the Jules Verne Challenge? Do *you* think she will?

8 🎧 **Listen to the radio broadcast about the Jules Verne Challenge. Were your predictions in Exercise 7 correct?**

Grammar focus

1 Study the examples of the present unreal conditional. Notice the ways to talk about hypothetical situations.

> If you **needed** more sleep, you **could** never **finish** the race.
>
> I **wouldn't** do it if I **were** scared of being alone.

2 Look at the examples again. Complete the rules in the chart with *the base form of the verb*, *the simple past form of the verb*, or *would*.

Present unreal conditional
Form the present unreal conditional with *If* + subject + _____ , subject + *would* or *could* + _____ .
If you are less certain, you can use *might* or *could* instead of _____ .
NOTE: Use *were* for all subjects when the verb in the *if* clause is *be*.

> *Grammar Reference page 145*

3 Rewrite these sentences using the present unreal conditional. Make any necessary changes.

1. It's too cold. We probably won't go swimming.
   If it weren't so cold, we'd go swimming.

2. I get lonely. I don't want to take part in a solo race.

3. You don't go out a lot. You don't meet many people.

4. I want to call her. I don't know her number.

5. John isn't here. I want to ask him about the weekend.

6. Marta is scared of small spaces. She won't use the elevator.

7. People don't always understand him. He talks too fast.

Pronunciation

4 🎧 Listen to these conditional sentences. Notice the weak and contracted forms of *would* and the weak pronunciation of *could*.

If it weren't so cold, we'd go swimming.

I wouldn't do it if I were scared of being alone.

If you needed more sleep, you could never finish the race.

5 🎧 Listen again and repeat. Then say the sentences you wrote in Exercise 3. Use contracted or weak forms where possible.

Speaking

6 *BEFORE YOU SPEAK.* Imagine being alone for 100 days on a deserted island. What three luxury items would you take with you?

7 *GROUPS OF 4.* Tell about the items you would take with you and why. Others in the group will ask questions and fill in the chart.

A: In Sook, what three items would you take?
B: I'd take a cell phone because . . .

Student's name	Luxury items
In Sook	a cell phone

8 Report to the class. Say one thing that surprised you about your classmates' answers.

In Sook would take a cell phone. That surprised me because she wouldn't be able to call anyone from so far away.

Writing

9 Imagine you are alone—in a solo yacht race, on a deserted island, or in another lonely situation. Imagine it is now day 50 of 100. Write a diary entry about what you would be doing and how you would feel.

CONVERSATION TO GO

A: If you **went** to a desert island, what **would** you **take**?
B: **I'd get** very lonely, so I think **I'd take** a friend!

Commuter blues

Vocabulary Expressions with *time*
Grammar Connectors: *although, despite (not), however, in spite of*
Speaking Comparing attitudes

Getting started

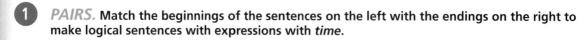

1 *PAIRS.* **Match the beginnings of the sentences on the left with the endings on the right to make logical sentences with expressions with *time*.**

1. He thinks commuting is a **waste** __i__   a. **the time** he gets home.
2. He always arrives at work **on** ____   b. **time for** dinner with his family.
3. He never gets home **in** ____   c. **time off.**
4. He'll have more **leisure** ____   d. **more time** with his family.
5. He always feels stressed **by** ____   e. **of time** until he retires.
6. He would like to **spend** ____   f. **time.**
7. He gets a lot of ____   g. **time** when he retires.
8. His commute **takes** ____   h. **a long time.**
9. It's just **a matter** ____   i. **of time.**

2 *PAIRS.* **Which sentences in Exercise 1 are true for you?**

64

Listening

3 🎧 **Listen to three people talk about traveling to work and school and complete the chart.**

Speaker	How does he/she get there?	How long does the trip take?	How does he/she feel about the trip?
1			
2			
3			

Reading

4 *PAIRS.* **Look at the photos and the title of the article. What do you think the article will say about Tadao Masuda, the man in the smaller picture?**

5 **Read the article and answer these questions.**

1. How long does Tadao spend traveling each day?
2. How does he feel about commuting?
3. How does he use the time on the train?

6 **Read the article again. Which of the sentences in Exercise 1 on page 64 are true for Tadao Masuda?**

Long-distance Commuter

So you think you have a difficult trip to work, with the traffic, heat, and mobs of people. You fight through crowds, down tunnels, up escalators. And you arrive at work sweaty and tired. However, it could be a lot worse.

Consider Tadao Masuda, who lives in Japan. His commute to work takes three and a quarter hours and then another three and a quarter back home again. He gets up at 4:00 A.M. Although he knows the commuting time to the minute, he leaves nothing to chance. He leaves at 4:55, gets on the train at 5:16, and always arrives in the office on time. He finally returns home at 8:50 in the evening, in time for dinner with his family. He knows his routine well—after all, he has been doing it for 30 years.

Despite not enjoying the trip, Tadao does not complain about it. "I don't actually enjoy commuting, but I definitely don't feel it is a waste of time. It is my private space, and I use this time for my own thoughts. I usually get home relaxed, despite the stress caused by a long day of hard work."

Today at age 65, he is considering a change. He would like to spend more time with his wife and family. In spite of staying with the same company all his life, he still gets only ten days off a year. However, will he be happy when he retires and ends his 30-year routine?

14

Grammar focus

1 **Study the examples of connectors. Notice the ways to express contrasting ideas.**

> You arrive at work tired. **However**, it could be a lot worse.
> **Although** he knows the commuting time to the minute, he leaves nothing to chance.
> I usually get home relaxed, **despite** the stress caused by a long day of hard work.
> **Despite** living only 10 miles from school, I have a pretty long commute.
> **Despite not** enjoying the trip, he doesn't complain about it.
> **In spite of** the noise and crowding, I'm glad I live in the city.
> **In spite of** staying with the same company all his life, he still gets only 10 days off a year.

2 **Look at the examples again. Complete the rules in the chart with *however, although, despite (not)*, or *in spite of*.**

Connectors: *although, despite (not), however, in spite of*
Use _____ and _____ before a noun or gerund.
Use _____ before a gerund.
_____ is often followed by a comma, then a complete sentence.
Use _____ to introduce a subject + verb clause when there is another clause in the sentence.

> *Grammar Reference page 145*

3 **Rewrite the sentences using the words in parentheses. Make any necessary changes.**

1. My commute is long. I enjoy living outside of the city. **(in spite of)**

   In spite of my long commute, I enjoy living outside of the city.

2. There was heavy traffic this morning. I got to work on time. **(despite)**

3. I don't really like my job. I need the money. **(however)**

4. I like my job. I don't like commuting. **(although)**

5. He is very busy. He manages to take some time off. **(despite)**

6. I leave on time. I'm always late. **(in spite of)**

7. He doesn't have an alarm clock. He always wakes up on time. **(despite not)**

8. I thought the interview went well. I didn't get the job. **(however)**

9. She works long hours. She has lots of energy. **(in spite of)**

10. It was raining hard this morning. I walked to work. **(although)**

Pronunciation

4 🎧 Listen to the examples in Exercise 1 on page 66. Notice the position of the commas in the sentences. How do the commas affect the pronunciation?

5 🎧 Listen again and repeat.

Speaking

6 *BEFORE YOU SPEAK.* Look at the ideas in the notebook in relation to your time. How do you feel about each one?

I have a long commute, and I don't enjoy it at all. The train is always crowded, so I never get a seat . . .

7 *PAIRS.* Discuss your notes. Ask and answer follow-up questions.

8 Report to the class. Did you have any different attitudes toward time?

- Your commute

- Your home or family life

- The time you have for fun and relaxation

- Your work or school schedule

Writing

9 Write a note to a friend describing your regular trip to school or work. Use connectors in your answers to these questions.

- How do you get there?
- What do you do while you're traveling?
- How long does it take?
- How do you feel about it?

CONVERSATION TO GO

A: **Although** I try to be **on time**, I'm often **late**.
B: Maybe you should get a wake-up service.

Small talk

Vocabulary Ways of talking
Grammar Tag questions
Speaking Making small talk

Getting started

1 *PAIRS.* **What are the people in the picture doing? What do you think they are discussing?**

2 Match the verbs and verb phrases in bold with the correct definitions.

1. We usually sit in the café for hours and **chat about** our experiences. __c__

2. I know Steve **talks about me behind my back**. Why doesn't he talk directly to me? ____

3. I hate to **gossip**, but Max and Liz just had a big fight. Everyone's talking about it. ____

4. Hillary **brags about** her family's money all the time. She's getting annoying. ____

5. Jim **bores me to tears** talking about his hobby, collecting insects. Who cares about insects? ____

6. All I do at work parties is **make small talk** and discuss the new reality TV shows. ____

7. He **complains about** his job all the time. Why doesn't he look for a new one? ____

8. Can I **confide in** you? You won't tell anyone my secret, will you? ____

a. make someone tired and impatient by talking about things he or she's not interested in

b. speak too proudly about what you have, what you've done, etc.

c. talk in a friendly, informal way

d. say that you are annoyed or unhappy about something or someone

e. tell someone about something private because you feel you can trust the person

f. talk about other people's private lives

g. have a conversation about unimportant topics

h. say negative things about others when they aren't present

3 *PAIRS.* **Look at the expressions in Exercise 2 again. What is the one thing you sometimes do? Never do?**

Reading

4 Read the column on how to be a good conversationalist. Add *Do* or *Don't* as appropriate before each tip.

Conversation *do's* and *don'ts*

Have you ever been to a party and found you had nothing to say? Try these top tips.

a. <u>Do</u> chat about vacations and leisure time—things we all have in common.

b. _____ make sure you know who you are confiding in, especially if you're gossiping or criticizing someone.

c. _____ simply ask questions that require only a *yes* or *no* answer. Ask follow-up questions that give the other person something to talk about.

d. _____ bore people to tears by complaining about some bad experience.

e. _____ make small talk. Read newspapers and watch the news. If you don't have time for books and movies, read the reviews.

f. _____ count to four in your head before interrupting someone. Otherwise, it sounds as if you couldn't wait for the other person to stop talking.

g. _____ get into deep conversations about your personal life.

Listening

5 🎧 Listen to six short conversations and match each one with the tips in Exercise 4. Note: Conversation 5 matches two tips.

1. <u>a</u>   2. _____   3. _____   4. _____   5. _____ and _____   6. _____

6 🎧 Listen again and complete the sentences.

1. The weather has been beautiful, _____<u>hasn't it</u>_____?

2. Well, you got some sun, _____?

3. It doesn't usually take long, _____?

4. That movie wasn't very good, _____?

5. That painting is awful, _____?

6. You're not the artist, _____?

7. You won't tell anyone, _____?

8. Times have changed, _____?

9. You live in this apartment building, _____?

10. It's a nice neighborhood, _____?

Grammar focus

1 Study the examples of tag questions. Notice the ways to ask for agreement or check information.

> It doesn't usually take long, **does it?**
> You're not the artist, **are you?**
> You got some sun, **didn't you?**
> The weather has been beautiful, **hasn't it?**
> The movie wasn't very good, **was it?**

2 Look at the examples again. Underline the correct words to complete the rules in the chart.

Tag questions
If the first part of the sentence is affirmative, the tag question is **affirmative / negative**.
If the first part of the sentence is negative, the tag question is **affirmative / negative**.
If the verb in the first part of the sentence is *be*, form the tag question with **be / do**.
If the main verb in the first part of the sentence is not *be*, form the tag question with **do / have**.
The verb tense in the first part of the sentence and in the tag question is **the same / different**.

Grammar Reference page 146

3 Write tag questions to complete these sentences.

1. It's been fantastic weather, _____*hasn't it*_____?

2. It was a long trip, _____?

3. They prepared all this food themselves, _____?

4. There isn't any more coffee, _____?

5. You don't happen to know where the restrooms are, _____?

6. She's in our English class, _____?

7. You will stay for dinner, _____?

8. They couldn't have forgotten, _____?

9. You haven't met my husband yet, _____?

10. You work with computers, _____?

Pronunciation

4 🎧 Listen to the first conversation from Exercise 5 on page 69. Notice that when the speaker is just asking for—and expecting—agreement, the intonation of the tag question falls at the end. When the speaker is asking a real question to check information, the intonation of the tag question rises at the end.

The weather has been beautiful, hasn't it?　　Well, you got some sun, didn't you?

5 🎧 Listen again and repeat.

6 🎧 Listen to the sentences you completed for Exercise 3 on page 70. Is the first speaker in each item just seeking agreement or asking a real question to check information? Mark the tag questions with rising or falling arrows.

1. It's been fantastic weather, hasn't it?

Speaking

7 *BEFORE YOU SPEAK.* Think of five classmates and one thing you know about each of them. What tag questions can you ask to check? Think about vacation plans, social life, family, or interests. Make notes.

8 Walk around the room. Talk to the five people you wrote about in Exercise 7. Start a conversation with each of them, asking a tag question.

A: Ann, you're going on vacation, aren't you?
B: Yes, that's right.

Name	Information
1. Ann	going on vacation next month
2.	
3.	
4.	
5.	
6.	

Writing

9 Write an email to a friend you haven't seen for a while. Catch up on your friend's news by asking questions. Find out what's new and ask how your friend's previous plans have turned out. Try to include some tag questions.

CONVERSATION TO GO

A: This is a great party, isn't it?
B: Yes! You didn't come to the last one, did you?

UNIT 16

A star is born ... or made?

Vocabulary Fame and success
Grammar Passive constructions
Speaking Describing a process

Lesson A

Getting started

1 *PAIRS.* **Look at the photos of famous people and the reviews of them. Do you agree?**

"The Spice Girls became very **popular** in the 1990s. Although some critics doubted they were very **talented**, the expectations were high for this group of **trendy** and **fashionable** young women. However, their success didn't last long, and they soon disappeared from the scene."

"Although boy band N'Sync did not start out as a **spectacular** success, their music and dancing caught on, and their albums were **sensational** hits, especially with pre-teen girls. Some say that only two of the five really sing when the group performs; others say their songs all sound the same."

"Macaulay Culkin is the perfect example of a child star who became a celebrity at an early age. But the question remains whether it is desirable for a child to be wealthy and **successful** at such an early age."

"Britney Spears is one of the most **influential** pop stars in recent memory. But let's face it: Britney's voice and dancing skills are **mediocre**."

2 *PAIRS.* **Look at the adjectives in bold in Exercise 1. Write the noun form for each adjective.**

Adjective	Noun	Adjective	Noun	Adjective	Noun
fashionable	fashion	popular		successful	
influential		sensational		talented	
mediocre		spectacular		trendy	

72

Pronunciation

3 🎧 Listen to the pairs of adjectives and nouns you wrote in Exercise 2 on page 72. Underline the stressed syllable in each word.

4 🎧 Listen again and repeat.

Reading

5 *PAIRS.* Discuss. Are you born a star or are you made a star? Explain your opinion.

6 Read the article about Britney Spears and answer these questions.

1. Who have Britney's biggest fans been?

2. What was her image when she first became a star?

3. According to the article, why is she so popular?

Britney, One More Time

Britney Spears has impeccable timing. She arrived on the pop music scene as a teenager in 1998, a time when the popular music industry was driven by young adolescents with plenty of money to spend. Dressed in her school uniform, she projected an image that was sweet, innocent, and self-confident. Unlike many young stars, Britney wasn't pushed into a career by her parents. Instead, she pushed herself. After two auditions, she was selected as a child actor on the "Mickey Mouse Club," a Disney TV show. Her first recording contract was signed when she was 15.

Two years later, her breakthrough album, "Baby One More Time," was released and never dropped out of the Top Ten for an entire year. So far, over 13 million copies of the album have been sold. Britney became a legend while still in her teens.

How is Britney's astonishing success explained? Aggressive marketing! Her face is seen everywhere, her music is heard everywhere, and recording companies go out of their way to reach the most powerful market segment in the United States today—pre-teens and teenagers, who identify with the lovesick themes of her songs.

What's next? Britney's music and dance are heavily influenced by her idol, Madonna. Britney and her teenage audience are growing up, and she is trying to reinvent herself—like Madonna—to keep her popularity alive. Will she succeed?

Listening

7 🎧 Listen to the radio program about the Spice Girls. How would the presenter answer the question, "Is a star born or made"?

8 🎧 Listen again. Write *T* (true) or *F* (false) after each statement.

1. A businessman created the Spice Girls in 1994.

2. At first, six Spice Girls were chosen.

3. Ginger Spice left the band to work for the United Nations.

Grammar focus

1 **Study the examples of active and passive sentences.**

Active sentences			Passive sentences		
Subject	**Verb**	**Object**	**Subject**	**Verb**	**Agent**
A businessman	**created**	the Spice Girls.	The Spice Girls	**were created**	by a businessman.
Madonna	**influences**	Britney's music.	Britney's music	**is influenced**	by Madonna.
They	**chose**	six Spice Girls.	Six Spice Girls	**were chosen.**	

2 **Look at the examples again. Underline the correct words to complete the rules in the chart.**

Passive constructions

In **active / passive** constructions, the subject is not the person or thing that does the action.

In passive constructions, the **agent / subject** may be unknown or not important.

Form the passive with *be* + the **base form / past participle** of the main verb.

Grammar Reference page 146

3 **Rewrite these sentences in the passive, making any necessary changes. Include the agent only when it is needed.**

1. The movie studio asked the actor to audition for the leading role in the movie.

   The actor was asked to audition for the leading role in the movie. (Agent not needed)

2. Madonna influences Britney Spears's music and dance.

3. The record company released the successful album *Skill* last year.

4. A reporter from *Time* magazine interviewed the new president.

5. The organizers always invite different celebrities to present the awards.

6. They need talented people for the TV show "American Idol."

7. Stunt men sometimes replace actors in dangerous scenes.

8. Ticket outlets sold 10,000 tickets for the concert in one hour.

9. The director gave the struggling actress a small part in the play.

10. Very often, parents push their children into acting careers.

Speaking

4 *PAIRS.* **How much do you know about pop queen Madonna? Take turns asking and answering questions to complete the missing information.**

Student A, look at page 136.
Student B, look at page 138.

A: When was she born?
B: In 1958.

5 *GROUPS OF 4.* **Without looking at your information, talk about what you found out about Madonna.**

A: Madonna was born in 1958 in Bay City, Michigan, USA.
B: You're right. And when did she start singing?
C: I think she started . . .

Writing

6 **Write a description of the process of producing a TV show, a music video, or a movie. Use the notes below and your imagination. Use the passive in some of your sentences.**

- hold auditions
- select performers
- scout locations
- design costumes
- hire the crew
- write and approve the script

CONVERSATION TO GO

A: How did the audition go?
B: Really well! In fact, I was chosen.
A: Congratulations!

Unit 13 Going it alone

1 Imagine yourself in the following situations. Think about how you would feel and what you would do or might do if these things happened to you.

- You are at home alone, asleep in the bedroom. The sound of breaking glass in the next room suddenly awakens you.

- A friend is driving you back home from a late-night party. There are other people in the car. It's a long way, and you don't think the driver is in a good condition to drive.

- You have an important job interview tomorrow, and you want to be at your best. It's 1 A.M. and you can't get to sleep.

- Your family wants to take a vacation at a beautiful resort 600 miles away. The best way to get there is by plane, but someone in your family is terrified of flying.

- You've just moved into a new apartment. The people next door have lots of friends over all the time and they're loud and rude. The noise disturbs you and even keeps you from sleeping.

- You move to a new town where you don't know anyone. You have no friends or family nearby.

2 *PAIRS.* Take turns talking about how you would react to the situations in Exercise 1. Give reasons for your responses. How do your answers compare?

Unit 14 Commuter blues

3 🎧 Listen to the conversation between a husband and wife about a job offer he has gotten. How does the husband feel about it? What does the wife think?

4 *PAIRS.* Have a debate about the two sides in the conversation. Use *however, although, in spite of,* and *despite (not)* to show contrasting ideas.

Student A's position

- Family is important, but a good job is essential.
- The husband needs to make a living and build a career.
- Commuting is a problem, but the advantages of the job are greater than the disadvantages.

Student B's position

- Spending time with family is more important than a job.
- A long commute can be stressful and bad for your health.
- The husband has a good opportunity, but making money isn't the most important thing in life.

Unit 15 Small talk

5  Listen to people at a party making small talk. Write down three questions you hear.

6 *GROUPS OF 5.* You are at a party. Use questions like the ones you wrote in Exercise 5 to make small talk.

Unit 16 A star is born . . . or made?

7 *PAIRS.* Ask and answer questions to complete the information about tennis stars Venus and Serena Williams.

Student A, look at page 137.
Student B, look at page 139.

8 *GROUPS OF 3.* Have a debate about the greatest sports figure of the last 20 years. Use passive constructions to discuss these points about your candidates.

- Nicknames people gave him or her
- Honors and awards he or she has received
- Sports writers who named him or her the best in the sport
- Commercials that feature him or her

What's in the fridge?

Vocabulary Food and cooking
Grammar Verb + infinitive and verb + gerund
Speaking Talking about food and cooking

Getting started

1 *PAIRS.* **Give examples of each pair of words or phrases.**

1. takeout / snacks

   A: takeout—chicken and vegetables
   B: snacks—peanuts

2. ingredients / a recipe

3. a meal / a dish

4. meat / cold cuts

5. fish / seafood

Takanori Kotani
from Japan

2 **Complete each sentence with a word from Exercise 1.**

1. I eat lunch at noon and dinner at 6:30, and sometimes I have ___snacks___ in the afternoon.

2. I have all the _____ I need to make cheesecake, but I don't know how to make it.

3. We like to have our big _____ in the evening. We always start with soup.

4. My favorite kind of _____ is steak.

5. Shrimp, lobster, and clams are examples of _____.

3 *PAIRS.* **Discuss these questions.**

Do you like to have snacks? If so, when and what kinds?

What's your favorite meal of the day? What do you like about it?

Pronunciation

4 🎧 **Listen. Notice the pronunciation of the vowel sound /i/ in the words in the first row and the vowel sound /ɪ/ in the words in the second row.**

eat	meal	seafood	evening	ingredients
big	dish	dinner	chicken	shrimp

5 🎧 **Listen again and repeat.**

6 🎧 **Listen to the sentences you completed for Exercise 2. Then practice saying the sentences in pairs.**

78

Listening

7 **PAIRS.** Look at the photos of two chefs at home and discuss these questions.

What do you think is in their refrigerators?
How much cooking do you think they do at home?

8 🎧 Listen to the chefs and check your answers.

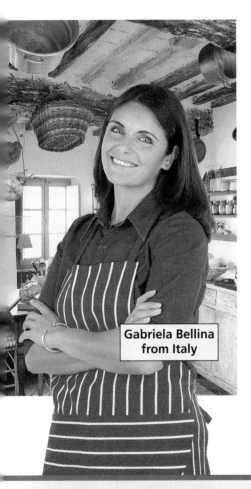

Gabriela Bellina
from Italy

9 🎧 Listen again. Write *Takanori* or *Gabriela* before each statement.

1. _____ thinks that chefs should be experimenting all the time.

2. _____ never eats at Italian restaurants.

3. _____ usually has the necessary ingredients for a sandwich at home.

4. _____ is interested in Chinese cuisine.

Reading

10 **PAIRS.** Look at the title of the article and discuss the three questions below the title.

11 Read the article. Write *T* (true) or *F* (false) after each statement.

According to the article:

1. many people eat snacks instead of meals.

2. about 42 percent of adults like to snack.

3. price is the most important consideration in choosing snacks.

4. snacking leads to weight gain.

Health forum

What Do We Really Eat?

How healthy is your diet? Do you spend much time cooking, or are you just too busy? Do you ever have snacks and fast food instead of full meals?

These are questions that many people are struggling with, and a recent survey shows that their answers aren't ideal. More and more people are choosing to snack throughout the day; in fact, snacks are replacing meals for a great number of people. Nine out of ten adults say they are snackers, and 42 percent say they snack at work. When they are on the go, many eat nutrition bars, peanuts, popcorn, or flavored drinkable yogurt in a bottle. People want to have foods that not only taste good, but are also easy to eat.

Snacks need to be convenient for consumers. The survey asked buyers the most important consideration in selecting snack foods. Nearly 70 percent said they prefer to buy ready-to-eat snacks.

The result of all this snacking? A lot of people don't know the difference between snacks and meals anymore. In most cases, the nutritional value of snacks is not very high. Instead, high fat and high calorie snack foods are common. Not surprisingly, nearly one-third of those surveyed are overweight, a significant health problem that no one can afford to ignore.

Grammar focus

1 **Study the examples of verbs followed by infinitives or gerunds.**

I've decided **to visit** some other countries.	I avoid **cooking** complicated dishes at home.
I don't often manage **to have** an evening off.	I spend time **relaxing** with friends.
You can't afford **to stand** still.	I've given up **trying** to keep my fridge neat.
Sometimes they offer **to do** the cooking.	I keep on **filling** the refrigerator.
I'm planning **to get** a larger fridge.	When I travel, I won't waste time **sightseeing**.

2 **Look at the examples again. Complete the rules in the chart.**

Verb + infinitive and verb + gerund

Some verbs must be followed by the infinitive, and some must be followed by the gerund.

Use the infinitive after these verbs: _____, _____, _____, _____, and _____.

Use the gerund after these verbs and verb phrases: _____, _____, _____, _____, and _____.

> Grammar Reference page 146

3 **Complete the sentences using the infinitive or gerund form of the verbs in parentheses.**

1. I'm planning _to learn_ (**learn**) how to cook.

2. I've decided _____ (**start**) exercising more so that I can eat all I want.

3. She wants to lose weight, but she can't give up _____ (**eat**) chocolate.

4. Even though we'd love to, we just can't afford _____ (**eat out**) every night.

5. I don't waste time _____ (**read**) recipes; I prefer my own ideas.

6. When I'm a guest at someone's home for dinner, I usually offer _____ (**do**) the dishes after the meal.

7. I avoid _____ (**go**) to restaurants where the service is bad.

8. On weekends, we spend time _____ (**shop**) and _____ (**cook**) exotic meals.

9. I take my lunch to work. I can't keep on _____ (**have**) pizza every day.

10. My friend manages _____ (**work**) all day, then comes home and does the cooking and the housework.

4 *PAIRS.* **Discuss. Which of the sentences in Exercise 3 are true for you?**

Speaking

5 *BEFORE YOU SPEAK.* **Read the questions in the survey. Add one more question of your own about people's food preferences.**

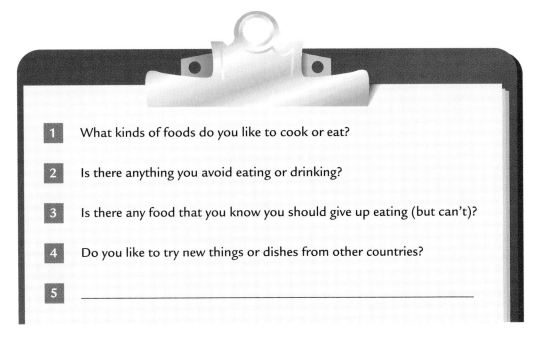

1 What kinds of foods do you like to cook or eat?

2 Is there anything you avoid eating or drinking?

3 Is there any food that you know you should give up eating (but can't)?

4 Do you like to try new things or dishes from other countries?

5 _____

6 *GROUPS OF 4.* **Take turns asking and answering the survey questions. Ask and answer follow-up questions. Take notes.**

A: *What kind of foods do you like to cook?*
B: *I like to cook rice, and I love eating it!*
C: *How do you prepare it?*

7 **Tell the class one interesting thing you found out about your classmates.**

Writing

8 **Write a description of what you usually cook and eat. Include details about what, where, when, and how. Also mention what you avoid eating.**

CONVERSATION TO GO

A: Do you spend much time cooking?
B: I avoid cooking, but I spend a lot of time eating!

Lesson A

Long walk to freedom

Vocabulary Words related to prison
Grammar Verbs for requirement, prohibition, and permission
Speaking Discussing freedom

Getting started

1 *PAIRS.* **Look at the photos and discuss these questions.**

What do the photos show?

Who is the man behind the bars? What do you know about him?

2 *PAIRS.* **Use the words in the box to complete the sentences about prison life.**

| ~~authorities~~ | cells | guards | life sentence |
| political prisoner | prisoners | privileges | supervision |

1. In prison, the _____authorities_____ make rules about the
    _____ that prisoners can have, such as exercise, mail,
    and visiting. Some inmates hardly ever leave their _____.

2. He is a _____. He was arrested because he criticized
    the government and he was given a _____ for his crime.
    He will never get out of prison.

3. There is strict _____ in the prison: The
    _____ are always watching the _____
    and controlling their movements.

Reading

3 *PAIRS.* **Discuss these questions about Nelson Mandela's time in prison at Robben Island.**

What rules do you think the prison had about writing and receiving letters?

How do you think Mandela reacted to the rules?

4 **Read the excerpt from Nelson Mandela's book *Long Walk to Freedom* about his time in prison. Were your predictions correct?**

5 **Read the excerpt again. What do you think Mandela meant by, "A letter was like the summer rain that could make even the desert bloom"?**

They only let me write one letter every six months. It was one of the facts of prison life. In prison, the only thing worse than bad news about one's family is no news at all. Mail was delivered once a month, and sometimes six months would go by without a letter. Often the authorities would keep mail out of spite. I can remember warders* saying, "Mandela, we have received a letter for you, but we cannot give it to you." No explanation of why, or who the letter was from.

When letters did arrive, they were cherished. A letter was like the summer rain that could make even the desert bloom. When I was handed a letter by the authorities, I would not rush forward and grab it as I felt like doing, but take it slowly. Though I wanted to tear it open and read it, I would not give the authorities the satisfaction of seeing my eagerness, and I would return slowly to my cell as though I had many things to occupy me before opening a letter from my family.

*warders (British English) = guards

Adapted from *Long Walk to Freedom*, by Nelson Mandela

Listening

6 🎧 **Listen to another excerpt from Nelson Mandela's book. Check (✓) the things he talks about.**

____ the cell ____ family ____ exercise ____ friends in prison

____ visits ____ food ____ letters ____ work

7 🎧 **Listen again and answer these questions.**

1. What type of prisoner was Nelson Mandela?
2. How long was his sentence?
3. What were the cells like?
4. What did the guards make prisoners do?
5. How long did the prisoners exercise?

8 *PAIRS.* **Discuss these questions.**

What do you think of the prison system that Nelson Mandela describes?

Was Mandela's treatment justified? Why?

Which freedoms are most important to you?

Grammar focus

1 Study the examples of *make*, *let*, and *be allowed to*. Notice the ways to express requirement, prohibition, and permission.

> A. They **made him work** in silence.
> B. They **let him write** a letter every six months.
> C. We **were allowed to exercise** for half an hour.
> D. They **didn't make him work** all day on Sundays.
> E. The guards **didn't let them exercise** in the morning.
> F. Prisoners **weren't allowed to touch** visitors.

2 Look at the examples again. Complete the rules in the chart with the letters of the examples.

Let, make, be allowed to
Sentence _____ expresses requirement (It was necessary.)
Sentence _____ expresses choice (It wasn't necessary.)
Sentences _____ and _____ express permission (It was OK to do something.)
Sentences _____ and _____ express prohibition (It wasn't OK to do something.)

> *Grammar Reference page 147*

3 Complete the sentences using the verbs in parentheses and the correct past form of *make*, *let*, or *be allowed to*. Add an object pronoun (*me, him, her*, etc.) if necessary.

1. There was a dress code at my school. We __weren't allowed to wear__ (wear) jeans.

2. Mandela's prison guards _____ (exercise) for only 30 minutes a day.

3. In the movie *The Shawshank Redemption*, prisoners were treated badly. Prison authorities _____ (work) long hours in the hot sun.

4. Our grandmother was very strict. She _____ (talk) at the dinner table.

5. My parents gave me no choice. They _____ (keep) my room neat and clean.

6. Mandela's life in prison was very difficult. They _____ (stay) in a very small cell.

7. Our family was very relaxed about rules — I _____ (come) home any time I wanted.

8. Some of Mandela's guards were kind. They _____ (work) when he was sick.

9. In my last job, they_____ (wear) my own clothes to work. I had to wear a uniform.

Pronunciation

4 🎧 **Listen. Notice the weak pronunciation of the object pronouns and the way the pronouns are sometimes linked to the word before them.**

They made us work in silence.

They didn't make me work all day on Sundays.

They let Kim write a letter every six months.

They didn't let us see our mail.

The guards didn't let them exercise.

They didn't let her visit Kim often.

5 🎧 **Listen again and repeat.**

Speaking

6 *BEFORE YOU SPEAK.* **Think about the times in your life when you had a lot of freedom. Think about other times when you had very little. Use the situations below or add your own ideas. Take notes.**

• family life   • school   • college   • a job   • a vacation   • military service

Most freedom	Least freedom
	Boarding school. They made me eat and sleep at designated times. And I also wasn't allowed . . .

7 *PAIRS.* **Discuss your experiences about freedom, using your notes. Ask each other follow-up questions.**

A: Can you think of a situation when you had very little freedom?
B: Boarding school was difficult. They made me get up at 6 A.M. and go to bed . . .

8 **Report on your partner's experiences about freedom.**

Writing

9 **Write about a historical figure or someone you know who experienced a lack of freedom. What was this person forced to do? What was this person not allowed to do? How did he or she overcome these difficulties?**

CONVERSATION TO GO

A: What rules did you have at school, Dad?
B: Well, the main one was we weren't allowed to enjoy ourselves.

Turning points

Vocabulary Things we read
Grammar Past perfect vs. past perfect continuous
Speaking Talking about important moments

Lesson A

Getting started

1 Match the words in the box with the statements.

a. an anthology	b. a bestseller	c. a biography
d. a column	e. an encyclopedia	f. a manual
g. ~~a novel~~	h. poetry/poems	i. a textbook

1. Two hundred pages of excitement.
    I almost believed it was a true story. _g_

2. This one contains classic short stories
    by some of the greatest authors. ____

3. I never read them . . . until a machine breaks
    down and then I need to fix it! ____

4. It's my favorite reference book. It has
    information about everything under
    the sun. ____

5. I enjoy reading the ones about
    political opinion. It's the first
    thing I read every day in the
    newspaper. ____

6. It was heavy, but the
    instructor said it was required
    for the course. ____

7. I like the imagery and the use
    of language. ____

8. That book has sold millions
    of copies! ____

9. I enjoy reading about the lives
    of famous people. ____

2 *PAIRS.* **Discuss these questions.**

What type of reading material do you read
most often?

When do you usually read?

What did you read, or what was read to you,
when you were a child?

Do you ever read a book and then see the
movie version of it? If so, which one is
usually better?

A suitcase

Reading

3 *PAIRS.* **What do you know about the author J. K. Rowling and the Harry Potter books?**

4 **Read the article and explain the article's title.**

5 **Read the article again and number these events in order.**

_____ a. worked as an English teacher   _____ f. wrote a story called "Rabbit"

_____ b. moved to Portugal   _____ g. became a bestselling writer

_____ c. worked as a French teacher   _____ h. had her first novel published

_____ d. studied French in college   _____ i. returned to the U.K.

_____ e. moved to Edinburgh

# of stories

J. K. Rowling (the *J* is for Joanne) is a best-selling British author. Her books are written for children, but adults love them too. In 1996, her big moment came when she heard that her first novel, *Harry Potter and the Philosopher's Stone,** would be published. "The moment I found out was one of the best of my life," says Joanne.

Before 1996, Joanne had been living in Portugal and teaching English. When she returned to the U.K., she had a suitcase of fantastic stories about a character named Harry Potter. She moved to Edinburgh and became a French teacher. It was there that she decided to finish the Harry Potter novel and get it published.

As a child, Joanne had always loved writing, and at age six, she had already finished her first story about a rabbit, called "Rabbit." From then on, she followed her love of languages. She enjoyed English at school and went on to study French in college.

Now that she has achieved her ambition, what does she say about writing? "Writing can be a lot of fun. It can also be a lot of hard work, but don't let that put you off! My advice to young writers is to read as much as you can, like I did. It will give you an understanding of what makes good writing and it will enlarge your vocabulary. Start by writing about things you know about—your own experiences and feelings. That's what I do."

***Note:** The title *Harry Potter and the Philosopher's Stone* was changed to *Harry Potter and the Sorcerer's Stone* when it was published in the U.S. and later made into a movie.

Listening

6 🎧 **Listen to a radio program about actor Daniel Radcliffe. What movie role made him famous?**

7 🎧 **Listen again and answer these questions.**

1. Had Daniel ever worked as an actor before the Harry Potter movies?

2. Why didn't his parents want him to become an actor?

3. What is he like, now that he is famous?

8 *GROUPS OF 4.* **Have you read any Harry Potter books or seen the movies? If so, what did you think of them?**

Grammar focus

1 **Study the examples of the past perfect and past perfect continuous tenses.**

> Before she was six, she **had finished** her first story. (past perfect)
> Before 1996, she **had been living** in Portugal. (past perfect continuous)

2 **Look at the examples again. Complete the rules in the chart with *past perfect* or *past perfect continuous*.**

> **Past perfect and past perfect continuous**
>
> Use the _____ to talk about an action or event that happened at a time before another action in the past.
>
> Use the _____ to talk about an activity or situation that continued for a period of time before another time in the past.

> *Grammar Reference page 147*

3 **Complete the sentences with the past perfect or the past perfect continuous of the verbs in parentheses.**

1. I didn't want to read the book because I _had already seen_ (**already / see**) the movie.

2. By the time his poetry was published in the anthology, he _____ (**write**) a hundred new poems.

3. Her eyes were red because she _____ (**study**) all night.

4. The bestseller *Lord of the Rings* became a very successful movie. Millions of people who _____ (**already / read**) the book went to see the film.

5. I _____ (**read**) the novel all evening and was halfway through it when I fell asleep.

6. One of my most embarrassing school experiences was when I gave an oral report about a book I _____ (**not / read**).

7. By the time we arrived at the theater, the movie _____ (**already / begin**).

8. The author _____ (**write**) the actress's biography for several years but he died suddenly, so he never managed to complete it.

9. When I got to the last page of the book, I realized that I _____ (**read**) it before.

10. Before becoming a novelist, he _____ (**work**) as a journalist for 10 years.

Pronunciation

4 🎧 **Listen. Notice that *had* and *been* usually have weak pronunciations.**

She had always loved writing.

She'd been living in Portugal.

She'd been working on the book for a long time.

By the time she was six, she had finished her first story.

She **had** a job teaching English.

She **had** a suitcase of stories.

5 🎧 **Listen again and repeat. When does *had* have a strong pronunciation?**

Speaking

6 *BEFORE YOU SPEAK.* **Think about three important events in your life. Make notes about the events and the background (what had been happening before then). Choose one of the situations below or think of another "turning point" in your life.**

- travel with friends for the first time
- get your driver's license
- go out on your first date
- get your first job

Important events/ turning points	Background
Went on a trip with two friends	Had always lived with my parents
	Had been traveling with my family before

7 *GROUPS OF 3.* **Share your stories about important moments in your life.**

When I was eighteen, I went on a trip with two friends. I had always wanted to travel on my own . . .

Writing

8 **Write about a moment or turning point in your life and explain the background.**

CONVERSATION TO GO

A: Why did you change jobs?

B: I'd been working there for 10 years and I was bored.

Looks good!

Vocabulary The five senses
Grammar Defining relative clauses
Speaking Defining people, things, time, and places

A

B

C

Getting started

1 Which of the five senses do you associate with each picture? Why?

hearing	sight	smell	taste	touch

2 *PAIRS.* Match the pictures to these sentences.

1. They taste delicious. E
2. It sounds like the sea.
3. It looks really beautiful.
4. It feels very smooth.

5. They smell very sweet.
6. It sounds strange.
7. It looks like a tropical island.

3 *PAIRS.* Look at the sentences in Exercise 2 and complete the rules with *an adjective* or *a noun*.

1. Use *feels, looks, smells, sounds,* or *tastes* before _____.
2. Use *feels like, looks like, smells like, sounds like,* or *tastes like* before _____.

Listening

4 🎧 Listen to four commercials. Which senses does each commercial suggest?

5 🎧 Listen again. Write *T* (true) or *F* (false) after each statement.

1. The toothpaste is made with ingredients that can be found in nature.
2. The morning is the time when most people will use the shower massager to relieve tension.
3. The perfume is appropriate for people who don't like to be noticed.
4. Port Royale is a place where you can treat most of your senses.

Pronunciation

6 🎧 Listen to the sentences. Notice the pronunciation of the *-s/-es* ending in the noun plurals and third person singular present tense verbs. Write each word in the correct column.

~~feels~~   ~~looks~~   tastes

flowers   smells   roses

breezes   fruits   beaches

sounds   birds   fragrances

/s/	/z/	/ɪz/
looks	feels	

7 🎧 Listen and check your answers. Then listen and repeat.

Reading

8 *PAIRS.* Predict. How do you think smells, such as lemon, coconut, and vanilla, affect people?

9 Read the ad to see if your predictions were right. Then read the ad again and answer these questions.

1. Which part of the brain do smells go to?

2. What are the three ways smells "work"? Give two examples of each.

3. Which smells would this company recommend for a library?

Smells That Work

It takes two seconds for a smell to enter your nose and travel to a part of the brain that controls memory and emotions. You probably do not realize what is making you hungry or suddenly calm.

Smells increase sales. Supermarkets use smells such as bread to make you want to buy. Travel agencies use coconut oil fragrances to persuade customers to travel to places where sunshine is the main attraction.

Odors help productivity. Some Japanese companies use lemon smells to increase energy during the work day and flower scents to improve concentration before and after lunch.

Fragrances are calming. A New York clinic that used the smell of vanilla found that patients who visited regularly reported a reduction in stress. Airlines put lavender smells in planes to relax people who are nervous. Even parents whose children are overactive find they can calm their kids down with certain scents.

Could smells help your business? If this is the idea you've been waiting for, then contact us today. Remember, this could be the day when your business experiences the sweet smell of success. Find out about smells that work!

Grammar focus

1 **Study the examples of defining relative clauses. Notice how defining relative clauses tell you which specific person, place, or thing the speaker means.**

> Smells travel to a part of the brain **that/which controls memory**.
> The smell of coconut brings to mind places **where sunshine is the main attraction**.
> Airlines put lavender smells in planes to relax people **who/that are nervous**.
> Parents **whose children are overactive** can calm their kids with certain scents.
> This could be the day **when/that your business experiences the sweet smell of success**.
> This is the idea **(that) you've been waiting for**.

2 **Look at the examples again. Complete the rules in the chart with** *that, when, where, which, who,* **or** *whose*.

Defining relative clauses
Use _____ to talk about places.
Use _____ or _____ to talk about people.
Use _____ or _____ to talk about time.
Use _____ or _____ to talk about things.
Use _____ to talk about people and their possessions.
NOTE: You don't need to use *who* or *that* when they are objects of the verb in the relative clause.

Grammar Reference page 147

3 **Combine the sentences. Add a relative pronoun (if necessary) and make any other changes.**

1. I remember the day. We met then.
   I remember the day when we met. OR
   I remember the day (that) we met.

2. There's that girl. She looks like your little sister.

3. That's the man. His daughter plays the clarinet.

4. I loved the smell of the flowers. You sent them to me.

5. I don't like those nightclubs. They play techno music there.

6. Did you like the CD? I lent it to you.

7. Do you remember the time? We stayed out all night then.

8. I really enjoyed the movie. We saw it on TV last night.

9. There's the teacher. Her book was published last year.

10. This is a picture of the resort. We spent our vacation there last summer.

Speaking

4 *BEFORE YOU SPEAK.* Think about each of the five senses. Think of your favorite thing for each one, for example, the sound of the sea. Can you also think of things you dislike, such as traffic noise?

Likes					
Dislikes					

5 *GROUPS OF 3.* Discuss your likes and dislikes. Ask and answer follow-up questions.

A: *I love the smell of grass that's just been cut.*
B: *Me too. But it's hard to find that smell in the city.*
C: *I know. In the city, I like the smell that comes out of the bakeries.*

Writing

6 Imagine a perfect place. Describe the sights, sounds, tastes, and smells of your perfect place. Use defining relative clauses, as appropriate.

CONVERSATION TO GO

A: I love the smell of bread that is still warm.
B: I prefer the taste!

Unit 17 What's in the fridge?

1 Read the article about eating out in the U.S. Answer these questions.

1. How often do people in the U.S. eat out?

2. Which meal do people skip most often?

3. Which groups of people eat out the most?

Eating Out in the U.S.

A new survey shows that people in the U.S. consume an average of 4.2 meals a week prepared outside the home, including restaurants and take-out. That figure is higher than it was 20 years ago, when the average was 3.7. While the number of meals prepared in the home has decreased, the number of meals people skip is on the rise, especially breakfast.

In general, men eat out more frequently than women, and people with higher incomes tend to eat out more than those who earn less.

---

2 *PAIRS.* Look at the statements. Are they true in your country (or in your family)? If not, change them to make them true for you.

- People like to eat out frequently.
- Very few people buy their lunch.
- Most people spend a lot of time cooking.
- A lot of people avoid eating breakfast.
- Most people frequently skip meals but manage to have dinner with family.
- Everyone enjoys taking friends out for dinner.

Unit 18 Long walk to freedom

3 🎧 Listen to two women talk about living in a college dormitory today compared with years ago. What has changed in the years since the mother lived in a dorm?

4 *PAIRS.* Take turns comparing your life as a child with your life today:

- How is your life today different from your life as a child?
- What did your parents make you do as a child that you don't have to do today?
- What did your parents let you do? What things weren't you allowed to do?
- Do you think your parents were wrong about any of the things they didn't let you do? Why?

Unit 19 Turning Points

5 Read the plot summary of *Harry Potter and the Sorcerer's Stone*. What happened to Harry when he was 11? What had happened before?

Harry Potter and the Sorcerer's Stone

Harry Potter led a hard life until he was 11 years old. His parents had died in a car crash when he was a baby (or so he thought).

Harry grew up with his aunt and uncle, who did not treat him well—they made him live under the stairs and his nasty cousin, Dudley, tormented him. Then, when Harry turned 11, he received a mysterious letter from the Hogwarts School of Witchcraft and Wizardry, informing him that he had been selected as a student. At this point,

Harry discovered the truth about his parents: His father had been a wizard and his mother had been a witch. They had been killed by an evil wizard while they were protecting Harry.

Harry's aunt and uncle had never told Harry the truth about his past, and now he was beginning to understand his destiny—the world of magic was where he belonged! Harry happily went to Hogwarts, where he met his teachers and made new friends to share his magical adventures.

6 Think of a book or a movie that you've read or seen that had an interesting story. Pick an important event in it. Make notes about the story and the background.

7 *PAIRS.* Take turns telling your stories. Start with the event and describe the background before that point.

Book or movie: _____
Event: _____
Place and time: _____
Four or five things that had happened or had been happening before the event:
_____
_____
_____
_____

What happened at the end? _____
_____

Unit 20 Looks good!

8 🎧 Listen to a TV game show, called "Who, Which, When?" Try to answer the questions while the clock is ticking. How many answers did you get right?

9 *PAIRS.* Now play the game.

Student A, look at page 140.
Student B, look at page 137.

10 *PAIRS.* Switch roles.

Student A, look at page 139.
Student B, look at page 140.

World of Music 3

Sad Songs (Say So Much)
Elton John

Vocabulary

1 *PAIRS.* **Match the phrases in bold with their definitions.**

1. We need to **iron out the rough spots.** ____
2. You should **tune in** to the music channels. ____
3. Your idea **makes sense.** ____
4. Bad weather really **gets to me.** ____
5. I **sing the blues** when I'm far from home. ____
6. Songs **say so much** about life! ____

a. causes a strong feeling
b. feel sad or sing a sad song
c. it's clear and easy to understand
d. make something difficult seem a little easier
e. they are very meaningful
f. watch a program on TV

*British singer-pianist **Elton John** (Reginald Kenneth Dwight) is one of the most widely recognized international music stars. Beginning with "Your Song" in 1970, he has been in the top 40 over 50 times. In 1993, Elton John surpassed Elvis Presley for having the most consecutive years of top 40 hits on Billboard's Hot 100.*

Listening

2 🎧 **Listen to "Sad Songs (Say So Much)," by Elton John. What is the main idea of the song? Circle the answer.**

a. Sad songs are the best kind of music.
b. Accepting and sharing your sadness is a way to feel better.
c. If you feel sad, you should sing a sad song.

3 🎧 **Listen again and complete the lyrics on page 97.**

Speaking

4 *GROUPS OF 3.* **Discuss these questions. Use lines from the song to explain your answer.**

1. Do you think the singer has ever felt sadness or suffered?
2. Why does the singer think it helps to listen to sad songs? Do you agree?
3. What does the singer mean by "It feels so good to hurt so bad"?
4. When you feel sad, do you to listen to music? If so, what kind of music?
5. What are your favorite sad songs? Do others in your group like the same ones?

Sad Songs (Say So Much)

Guess there are times ____

we all need to share a little pain,

And ironing out the rough spots

Is the hardest part when memories remain.

And it's times like these ____

we all need to hear the radio

'Cause from the lips of some old singer

We can share the troubles we already know.

____ 'em ____ ,

____ 'em ____ ,

____ ____ those sad songs.

When all hope is gone,

Why don't you ____ ____ and ____ them ____ .

They reach into your room,

Oh, just feel their gentle touch.

When all hope is gone,

Sad songs say so much.

If someone else is sufferin' enough, oh, to

____ it ____ ,

When every single word makes sense,

Then it's easier to have those songs around.

The kick inside is in the line finally

____ ____ you.

And it feels so good to hurt so bad

And suffer just enough to sing the blues.

So, ____ 'em ____ , ____ 'em ____ ,

____ ____ those sad songs.

When all hope is gone,

Why don't you ____ ____ and ____ them ____ .

They reach into your room

Oh, just feel their gentle touch.

When all hope is gone,

You know, sad songs say so much.

Sad songs, they say

Sad songs, they say

Sad songs, they say

Sad songs, they say so much.

So, ____ 'em ____ , ____ 'em ____ ,

____ ____ those sad songs.

When all hope is gone,

Why don't you ____ ____ and ____ them ____ .

They reach into your room

Oh, just feel their gentle touch.

When all hope is gone,

You know, sad songs say so much.

When all hope is gone,

You know, sad songs say so much.

When every little bit of hope is gone,

Sad songs say so much.

When every little bit of hope is gone,

Sad songs say so much.

Just looking

Vocabulary Shopping and sales techniques
Grammar Indefinite pronouns
Speaking Buying and selling

Lesson A

Getting started ━━━━━━━━

1 *PAIRS.* **Look at the photos and discuss these questions.**

What are the people doing?

What do you think they are saying?

2 *PAIRS.* **Complete the sentences with the words in the box.**

bait and switch	coupons	exaggeration
out of stock	~~rebate~~	package deal
fine print	loss leader	warranty

1. My new printer cost $79, but I sent in a form for a
   _____rebate_____, and I got $20 back.

2. Milk is a _____ in that store; they offer it at
   a low price just to get you inside.

3. The inserts in the Sunday newspaper are full of
   _____ that give you 50¢ or even $1.00 off
   lots of supermarket and drugstore items.

4. Most computers come with a one-year _____.
   If anything goes wrong, they repair it.

5. I signed the agreement without reading the _____
   closely. That was a mistake!

6. I tried to get the textbook at the bookstore, but it was
   _____. I'll try to buy it online.

7. The salespeople said the advertised item was sold out, and tried to
   sell me something more expensive. It was a _____!

8. The ad says this stereo is the best in the world. I think that is an
   _____.

9. I bought a lot of computer software in a _____,
   but I really use only two programs.

3 *PAIRS.* **Look at the sentences in Exercise 2. Have you had any experience with these practices? Explain.**

Reading

4 Read the article quickly and match the headings with the correct paragraphs.

> **Deception**

> **High-pressure tactics**

> **Overblown claims**

> **Come-ons**

Friendly Persuasion

Companies, stores, and salespeople use various techniques to get you to buy. Here are some common ones.

1. _____

- **Coupons.** Coupons may not always save you money, especially if you weren't planning to buy anything advertised in the coupon book beforehand.
- **Rebates.** Rebates only work if you remember to send in the rebate coupon.
- **Package deals.** Check to see if you really need everything in the package or if you're paying for items you wouldn't normally buy.
- **Loss-leaders.** You're lured into a store for a 15 percent discount to find yourself buying something you hadn't intended to purchase.

2. _____

- **Fine print.** Always check the fine print. You may find something you didn't expect.
- **Bait and switch.** A seller may advertise a special price, but when you come in, the item is out of stock. Then they try to sell you something more expensive.
- **Add-ons.** "Batteries not included." "Plus shipping and handling." Make sure you know the total price of everything you need to use a product.

3. _____

- **Claiming to be "the best."** Sometimes it doesn't matter if it's the best. It's more important that it works for you.
- **Obvious exaggerations.** A company may claim that "everybody loves" their product. Did they ask *everybody*?

4. _____

- **Deadlines.** "One day only, once in a lifetime!" "From 6 A.M. to 9 P.M." These are sales techniques that work to entice you to buy now.
- **Limited offers.** "Only while supplies last!" Did anyone tell you they have more than enough? "Only two left!" No one mentioned they only started with two.

Adapted from: http://www.mymoneyskills.com/visa VISA Card

5 Read the article again. Write *T* (true) or *F* (false) after each statement.

1. If something is advertised on sale and the store is out of stock, the seller will always offer you something else at a discount.

2. Buying more than one thing in a "package deal" is generally a great way to save money.

3. Using coupons can sometimes cost you money.

4. If there are only a few items left, it means a lot of people have bought the product.

Listening

6 Listen to three conversations between salespeople and customers. Write the number of the conversation next to the sales technique in Exercise 4 that matches it.

Grammar focus

1 **Study the examples of indefinite pronouns.**

> You won't find **anything** like it at other stores.
> Did **anyone** tell you about our big sale?
> **Everybody** thinks he or she is a good buyer.
> Would you like **something** to drink?
> **Anything** you've got will be fine.
> **No one** has returned any of these sofas yet!

SOFA SALE

2 **Complete the list of indefinite pronouns.**

	every-	some-	any-	no-
Object:	_____	something	_____	_____
	_____	somebody	_____	no one
Person:	everybody	_____	_____	_____

3 **Look at the examples again. Underline the correct words to complete the rules in the chart.**

Indefinite pronouns

Indefinite pronouns refer to people and things; they **name / don't name** exactly who or what.

When an indefinite pronoun is the subject, it takes a **singular / plural** verb.

Use **singular / plural** pronouns and possessive adjectives with indefinite pronouns.

Use indefinite pronouns starting with **any- / every-** in questions and negative sentences.

Use indefinite pronouns starting with **no- / some-** to make an offer to other people.

NOTE: In conversation and informal writing, indefinite pronouns are sometimes used with *they* or *their*: **Everyone** likes **their** cars.

Grammar Reference page 148

4 **Underline the correct words to complete the sentences.**

1. Everyone **love / loves** these TV sets. Would you like a demonstration?
2. Is there **anything / everything** I can help you with?
3. I've read the fine print in the warranty. Everything **look / looks** OK.
4. I have **nothing / everything** to do. Why don't we go shopping?
5. This printer is the best. You won't find **something / anything** better anywhere.
6. **Do / Does** anyone in your house like sports cars?
7. I'm sorry, but that item is out of stock. But I have **something / anything** else you might like.

Pronunciation

5 🎧 **Listen. Notice the stress in the indefinite pronouns.**

Everyone loves these.

Would you like **som**ething to drink?

Everybody is raving about them.

No one has returned them.

I'm afraid there's **no**thing I can do.

You won't find **an**ything like it.

6 🎧 **Listen again and repeat. Which part of the pronoun has the stress?**

Speaking

7 *BEFORE YOU SPEAK.* **Imagine you are a store salesperson. First think of three types of products or services you will be selling. Then make signs for your products and display them for your classmates to see.**

8 **Walk around the class and try to find the best deal for something you want to buy. Ask and answer follow-up questions.**

A: *I'm looking for something to give my 15-year-old nephew for his birthday.*
B: *We're having a sale on video games today. You won't find anything cheaper.*

Writing

9 **Imagine that you have bought a product or service, and you now feel that a salesperson or company used unfair or deceptive techniques to convince you to buy it. Write a letter of complaint. As appropriate, use indefinite pronouns.**

Write to one of these groups:
• a local consumer affairs association
• the company you made the purchase from

CONVERSATION TO GO

A: Is there anything I can help you with?
B: I want to buy something special for my sister's 21st birthday.
A: I think I have something she'll like.

Shaking hands

Vocabulary Doing business
Grammar Future real conditional and present unreal conditional
Speaking Talking about possible and unlikely/imaginary situations

Lesson A

Getting started

1 *PAIRS.* **Look at the pictures and discuss these questions.**

What kind of place are the people in? What are they doing?

2 *PAIRS.* **Match the columns to make logical sentences.**

1. I called ahead to **set up** __j__
2. We couldn't **reach** __c__
3. Our company **does** ____
4. We **consult (with)** ____
5. We hope to **negotiate** ____
6. We **scheduled** ____
7. We shook hands and **exchanged** ____
8. I often **go** ____
9. Every month I try to **make** ____
10. In business you have to **take** ____

a. **our sales reps** frequently.
b. **a meeting** with the sales director.
c. **an agreement** for a few days.
d. **contact** with important clients.
e. **on business trips**.
f. **a deal** that will satisfy everyone.
g. **risks** some of the time.
h. a lot of **business** in Brazil.
i. **business cards**.
j. **an appointment**.

3 *PAIRS.* **Use the expressions in bold in Exercise 2 to make sentences about yourself or people you know.**

I'd like to schedule a meeting with the instructor to discuss my progress in the course.

Reading

4 *GROUPS OF 3.* Do you know of any business customs in your country (or a country you have visited) that are different in other countries? What are they and how do they differ?

5 Take the quiz about business customs around the world. Check (✓) *T* (true) or *F* (false) after each statement. You will hear the answers in Exercise 6.

How do you do business around the world?

Try this quick quiz to test your business knowledge.   T   F

1. It's common to be offered coffee or mint tea in offices in the Middle East.   ☐ ☐
2. People rush business in Turkey.   ☐ ☐
3. In Spain, if a business associate invites you to dinner, it will be very late in the evening.   ☐ ☐
4. In the U.K. many people have business lunches in pubs.   ☐ ☐
5. Business lunches in Latin America usually last a short time.   ☐ ☐
6. In the U.S. most business lunches are long and leisurely.   ☐ ☐
7. You should make sure you're not late for a meeting in Singapore.   ☐ ☐
8. In South Korea you should give your business card with both hands.   ☐ ☐
9. If you give a gift to a business colleague in Thailand, the recipient will open it immediately.   ☐ ☐
10. Businesspeople in the U.S. will probably use first names as soon as they meet.   ☐ ☐

Listening

6 Listen to an interview with a business consultant and check your answers to Exercise 5.

7 *PAIRS.* Listen again and discuss these questions.

What business custom surprised you the most? Why?

Which business customs would you feel most comfortable with? Most uncomfortable?

Grammar focus

1 Look at the examples of the future real conditional and the present unreal conditional. Underline the verbs in the future real conditional sentences. Circle the verbs in the present unreal conditional sentences.

> You**'re not going to have** problems **if** you **travel** close to home.
>
> **If** you **have** a business lunch, it **will be** leisurely and relaxed.
>
> **If** I **visited** an office there, they **would offer** me a hot drink.
>
> I **would expect** a long meeting **if** I **wanted** to negotiate a deal there.

2 Look at the examples again. Complete the rules in the chart with *future real conditional* or *present unreal conditional*.

Future real conditional and present unreal conditional
Use the _____ to describe situations that will possibly happen under certain conditions.
Use the _____ to describe situations that are unlikely or imaginary.
Use the simple present in the *if* clause and *will* or *going to* + the base form of the verb in the result clause of _____ sentences.
Use the past tense form in the *if* clause and *would* + the base form of the verb in the result clause of _____ sentences.

Grammar Reference page 148

3 Decide whether each of these situations is likely or unlikely. Write sentences saying what you will do or would do in each situation.

1. A friend invites you for coffee after class.

   If a friend invites me for coffee after class, I'll say yes. (likely) OR

   If a friend invited me for coffee after class, I'd say yes. (unlikely)

2. Someone you've just met invites you to dinner.

3. A friend asks you to give his nephew a job.

4. You need to get a new job this year.

5. You're an hour late for an important meeting.

6. They offer you an excellent job in a foreign country.

7. You apply for a job that requires good English.

8. Your boss asks you to go on a business trip to Hawaii.

4 *PAIRS.* Compare your answers to Exercise 3. Are any of your answers different because you thought differently about whether the situations were likely or unlikely?

Pronunciation

5 🎧 **Listen. Notice the intonation in these conditional sentences.**

If you give someone a **gift**, you should use both **hands**.

If I visited an **of**fice, they would offer me a hot **drink**.

If you have a **bus**iness lunch, it will be leisurely and re**laxed**.

If you kept an ex**ec**utive waiting, it would be an **in**sult.

6 🎧 **Listen again and repeat.**

Speaking

7 *PAIRS.* **Ask and answer questions about possible and hypothetical situations. First decide if the situation is possible or unlikely, then ask the question.**

Student A, look at page 136.
Student B, look at page 140.

A: *What would you do if your boss didn't let you take a vacation for a year?*
B: *I'd be very upset. I'd probably look for another job.*

Writing

8 Write a list of do's and don'ts for international businesspeople visiting your country. Use the ideas in the list to help you. Use the future real conditional and the present unreal conditional as appropriate.

Business meetings
Punctuality
Business meals
Negotiating

CONVERSATION TO GO

A: What would you do if your boss asked you to go on a business trip to Hawaii?
B: I'd get on a plane before she changed her mind.

Growing up

Vocabulary Phrasal verbs related to growing up
Grammar Separable vs. inseparable phrasal verbs
Speaking Talking about growing up

Getting started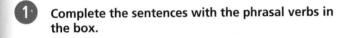

1 Complete the sentences with the phrasal verbs in the box.

bring up	~~get away with~~	look up to	make up
think over	look forward to	count on	pick on

1. Do you think kids these days __get away with__ too much?

2. I used to _____ stories all the time when I was little.

3. It's tough for children when other kids _____ them in school.

4. Most parents _____ their kids the best they can, but it isn't easy.

5. Children often _____ their older brothers or sisters.

6. I didn't start to _____ my career plans until I was in college.

7. It's important for teenagers to have someone they can _____.

8. Adolescents _____ becoming adults. Adults wish they were adolescents again.

2 *PAIRS.* Match the words with the pictures of different stages of life.

1. adolescent/teenager __A__   2. adult _____   3. child/kid _____

4. toddler _____   5. senior citizen _____

Listening

3 🎧 Listen to two people talk about stages of growing up. Complete the first row of the chart. Then listen again and complete the rest of the chart.

	Alex	Marie
Stage of growing up they talk about		
Ideas or events they discuss		
Relatives they talk about		
Kind of relationship they had		

4 *PAIRS.* Discuss. Which stage is the best and the worst? Why?

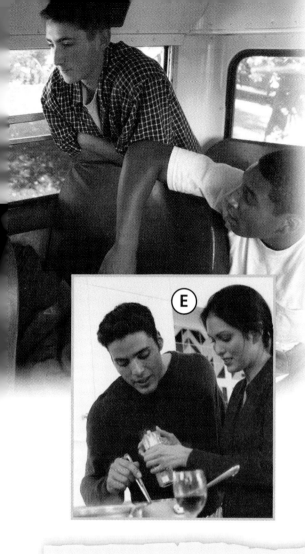

Reading

5 Whose job is easier, the parent of a young kid or the parent of an adult? Why?

6 Read the article quickly. Which paragraph describes

"the victim parent"____
"the can't let go parent" ____
"the silent parent"____

7 Read the article again and answer these questions.

Which type of parent would . . .

1. call his or her 30-year-old son to ask him if he had had dinner?

2. not talk to his or her adult daughter for a week because she decided to go on a trip?

3. complain to his or her son and say he doesn't spend enough time with his parents?

Parenting Adult Children

Almost everyone agrees: bringing up children is not an easy task. But does it get easier when the children grow up? Here is what parents and adult children say about different roles that parents sometimes play.

1. "I feel that I can't count on my children anymore. I understand they're adults, but they're still my children. I admit that sometimes I act like I need them to take care of me more than I really do. I also exaggerate a little bit when I don't feel well. I think they realize that I sometimes make up stories about needing them to help me around the house, but they don't say anything."

2. "When my father disagrees with any decision I make, he won't argue with me or even voice his opinion. Instead, he withdraws and stops talking to me. I'd rather discuss the situation than go through this game, but that's the way it is with him."

3. "I'm in my first year of college, and I'm living away from my parents for the first time. It's hard for me, and I know it's hard for them, too. But I'm afraid they haven't figured out yet that I'm an adult and that I don't need to be supervised all the time. It sounds funny when I say it, but they call me to ask if I'm getting enough to eat or if I remembered to wear a coat when it's cold."

Grammar focus

1 Look at the examples of separable and inseparable phrasal verbs. Underline the direct object in each sentence.

Separable phrasal verbs	Inseparable phrasal verbs
I'm used to **figuring** things **out** for myself. She knew when I was **making up** stories. They tried to **bring** me **up** properly.	We used to **pick on** the younger kids. I really **looked up to** him. I had **turned into** the boring old parent. They **got away with** stuff.

2 Look at the examples again. Underline the correct information to complete the rules in the chart.

Separable vs. inseparable phrasal verbs

Phrasal verbs consist of two or more words: a verb and one or two particles, like *up* or *away*.

With **separable / inseparable** phrasal verbs, the direct object *must* follow the phrasal verb.

With separable phrasal verbs,

- if the direct object is a **noun / pronoun**, it can go between the parts of the phrasal verb or it can follow the phrasal verb.

- if the direct object is a **noun / pronoun**, it must go between the parts of the phrasal verb.

Grammar Reference page 148

3 Complete the sentences with the correct form of the words in parentheses. Remember to write the object between the parts of the phrasal verb when necessary. More than one correct answer is possible in some cases.

1. I used to love summer vacations. I _looked forward to them_ (look forward to/them) every year.

2. My parents were very lenient, but they never let me _____ . (get away with/misbehaving in school)

3. When we were kids, my older sister always _____ . (pick on/me)

4. Most parents want to _____ (bring up/their children) well.

5. She has always _____ . (look up to/her mother)

6. I don't understand my sister at all. I can't_____ . (figure out/her)

7. My dad is very calm. I know I can _____ (count on/him) in a crisis.

8. He was weak and thin as a kid, but he _____ (turn into/an athlete) when he grew up.

9. Thank you for your advice. I'm going to _____ . (think over/it)

10. My brother used to play loud music when I was studying. I finally got him headphones because I couldn't _____ (put up with/the noise) anymore.

Pronunciation

4 🎧 **Listen. Notice the stress in the phrasal verbs.**

Growing up is **figuring** things **out** for yourself.   Don't believe that. He probably **made** it **up**.

I don't know how my parents **put up with** me.   I **get along with** them well now.

I knew I could **count on** her.   We used to **pick on** them.

5 🎧 **Listen again and repeat.**

6 **Underline the information to complete the rules.**

1. Most phrasal verbs have stress on the **verb / particle**.

2. However, inseparable phrasal verbs with one particle often have stress on the **verb / particle**.

3. Phrasal verbs with two particles have stress on the **first / second** particle.

Speaking

7 *BEFORE YOU SPEAK.* **Look at the questions in the chart and think about your own answers.**

8 *GROUPS OF 3.* **Discuss the questions in Exercise 7. Ask and answer follow-up questions. Do you all have similar opinions and experiences? What is one thing that you all have in common?**

A: When I was younger, I looked up to my older sister.
B: Why?
A: Well, she was really smart in school, and she was also very popular. I could always count on her to help me out if I had a problem.

- Did you look up to anyone when you were younger? Who? Why?

- Did anyone pick on you in school? Who?

- As a child, what kinds of things did you look forward to when you grew up? Why?

- What kinds of things did you find hard to put up with in school? Has this changed for you now?

Writing

9 **Write a short description of an important event or person in your life when you were growing up. Use some of the phrasal verbs from this unit, as appropriate.**

CONVERSATION TO GO

A: Growing up isn't so easy. You need someone to look up to.
B: I'm the tallest in my family, so I don't look up to anyone!

UNIT 24

Neat and clean

Vocabulary Household chores, errands, and services
Grammar Passive causatives: *have something done*; reflexive pronouns
Speaking Talking about things you do yourself and things you have
done for you

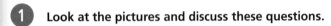

Getting started

1 **Look at the pictures and discuss these questions.**

1. What is the man doing?
2. What do you think the girl and her mother are
talking about?

2 **Underline the correct word in each sentence related
to housework, chores, and home services.**

1. We usually **do / have** the grocery shopping on weekends.
2. I try to keep my closets neat. I **paint / organize** them
at least twice a month.
3. Do you **make / do** all the housework yourself?
4. Do you know how to **install / fix** a broken pipe?
5. We have the newspaper **delivered / sold** to our door
on weekends.
6. I hate **making / doing** the ironing. I wonder if there's
anyone who likes it?
7. It's best to have a big party **catered / served**. The
preparations are too much work for one person.
8. It costs too much to have my car **washed / repaired**.
I usually fix it myself.
9. The person who **makes / does** the cooking shouldn't
make / do the dishes afterward.

3 *PAIRS.* **Discuss these questions.**

Which of the sentences in Exercise 2 do you agree with, or are true for you?

Which chores and errands does someone else do for you?

Which chores do you like or dislike doing?

Reading

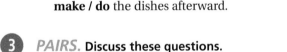

4 *PAIRS.* **Read the first paragraph of the advertisement for "Service with a Smile."
Predict. What kinds of services do you think they offer?**

5 Read the rest of the ad and match the headings with the correct paragraphs in the ad. Were your predictions correct?

- Errand and delivery services
- Shopping special
- Meal preparation
- Housekeeping services
- Party planning

Service with a Smile
Services in your home and beyond

Service with a Smile understands that you can't do everything yourself. You have a busy life, you work hard, and you'd like to have all the boring, tedious things done by somebody else. Sound familiar? Then read on . . .

1. _____

No time to do all the housework yourself? Have your housecleaning, laundry, and ironing done while you're at work—*Service with a Smile's* housecleaning service is quick and efficient, and it's reasonably priced.
"After our daughter's 21st birthday party, the house was a complete mess, but luckily I had it cleaned by *Service with a Smile's* special 'party cleanup' service."
Sue Lloyd, Seattle

2. _____

Why do all the cooking yourself? You can have gourmet meals delivered to your door. Tell us your preferences, and your personal chef will prepare exceptional dishes.
"The meals are fabulous! I couldn't do better myself."
L. Chaves, Boston

3. _____

Too busy to run all those errands? No problem. We'll pick up the dry cleaning, return the movie rentals and library books, and even wait in line to buy tickets at the box office for you.
"Without *Service with a Smile* I would never be able to do all my errands on time!"
John Park, Miami

4. _____

Like cooking but can't stand going to the supermarket? Have your weekly shopping done for you. You can email us your shopping list, and we'll have all your groceries delivered at the time you choose.
"I've been using *Service with a Smile* for years now—it means I don't have to deal with long lines at the supermarket after work."
M. Zhang, Toronto

5. _____

Need help planning a party? We can cater your party and take care of all the details! Enjoy the festivities and leave the worrying to us!
"They took care of everything, down to the tiniest detail."
Maria Lopez, El Paso

Listening

6 🎧 Listen to people talk about things they need to do. Write the number of the conversation next to each heading in Exercise 5.

111

Grammar focus

1 Look at the examples of passive causatives and reflexive pronouns. Check (✓) the passive causative sentences and underline the reflexive pronouns. See the Grammar Reference on page 149 for a list of reflexive pronouns.

Have all your **washing and ironing done**. You can't do everything **yourself**.	You can **have** your **meals delivered** to your door. I like to do the cooking **myself**.

2 Look at the examples again. Underline the correct answers to complete the rules in the chart.

Passive causatives and reflexive pronouns

Use the passive causative to say that **someone does something for you / you do something yourself**.

The subject and the reflexive pronoun refer to **a different / the same** person or thing.

> *Grammar Reference page 149*

3 Complete the conversations. Use the correct form of the passive causative in one part, and use a reflexive pronoun in the other part.

1. A: Would you ever ___have your laundry done___ **(laundry/do)** for you?

   B: No, I'd rather _____do it myself_____.

2. A: Did you _____ **(hair/cut)**? It looks great!

   B: I _____. Thanks.

3. A: My car is really dirty, but I don't want to _____ **(wash/it)**.

   B: Why don't you _____ at that new car wash? They're great!

4. A: My bike is broken. I usually _____ **(repair/it)**, but I don't have the time.

   B: I _____ at The Spoke Shop last week. They did a good job.

5. A: Did you _____ **(house/paint)**? The new colors look great.

   B: Actually, we _____. We did it during our vacation.

6. A: Do you _____ **(gifts/wrap)** when you buy them at a department store?

   B: Only if there's no extra charge. Otherwise, I _____.

Pronunciation

4 🎧 Listen. Notice the way the focus word in each sentence or clause stands out. The voice jumps up or down on this word and the vowel sound is long and clear.

A: Would you ever have your **laun**dry done for you?

B: **No**, I'd rather do it my**self**.

5 🎧 Listen to the short conversations you completed for Exercise 3. Then listen again and repeat.

Speaking

6 **BEFORE YOU SPEAK.** Write three things you would like to have done for you and three things you prefer to do yourself. Use these ideas or others of your own.

- Errands
- Spa services (massage, facial)
- Home maintenance and improvement
- Clothes (shopping, laundering, tailoring)
- Deliveries (meals, laundry, groceries)
- Personal grooming (nails, hair)
- Car maintenance
- Pet services

7 **GROUPS OF 3.** Compare your notes. Ask and answer follow-up questions.

A: *What things would you like to have done for you?*
B: *I'd like to have my car washed every week.*

Writing

8 Write a paragraph describing the services you would use if you were extremely rich. Is there anything you would still do yourself? Use the passive causative and reflexive pronouns as appropriate.

CONVERSATION TO GO

A: Do you ever **have** your hair **done**?
B: No, I do it **myself**.

Unit 21 Just looking

1 Look at the chart. Fill in the blanks in the first column with a kind of store. Then fill in the "Student A" column with things you have bought recently for each shopping option. If you did not use a shopping option, put an *X* in the chart.

Shopping options	Student A	Student B	Student C	Student D
a _____ store				
a TV shopping network				
a mail-order catalog				
an online _____ store				

2 *GROUPS OF 4.* Take a survey. Find out how each person in your group shops. Write down an example of what the person bought.

3 *GROUPS OF 4.* Discuss these questions about your group.

Which way has everyone shopped?
Which way has no one shopped?
Is there any item that everyone has bought?
Has anyone bought something at all of the places? Who?

Unit 22 Shaking hands

4 🎧 Listen to the conversation between two friends. What are their ideas about free time?

5 Think about what you will do if you get some free time and what you would do with all the time in the world. Fill in the chart with your ideas.

If I have some free time this evening / this weekend / later this year . . .	If I had all the time in the world . . .

6 *PAIRS.* Compare your ideas from Exercise 5.

Unit 23 Growing up

7 🎧 Listen to two longtime friends talk about their childhoods. What do they remember?

8 *GROUPS OF 3.* Take turns talking about your own childhood memories. Have you had similar experiences?

Unit 24 Neat and clean

9 Look at the list of services provided by "Lend-a-Hand Services." Which services would you like to have done for you?

Lend-a-Hand Services

A helping hand when you need it!

Services:

- ❏ Housecleaning
- ❏ Laundry & ironing
- ❏ Organizing closets
- ❏ Grocery shopping
- ❏ Meal delivery
- ❏ Laundry pickup & delivery
- ❏ DVD/Video rentals & returns

- ❏ Plant care & watering
- ❏ Gift shopping & wrapping
- ❏ Car wash or repair
- ❏ Pharmacy pickup
- ❏ Party catering
- ❏ Babysitting
- ❏ Hairstyling & nails

10 *PAIRS.* Role-play a customer and a pushy salesperson from "Lend-a-Hand Services." Take turns.

UNIT 25

A winning formula

Vocabulary Words related to business processes
Grammar Nondefining relative clauses
Speaking Describing business plans

Getting started

1 Complete the chart with the correct form of the nouns or verbs.

Noun	Verb
an ad / advertisement	advertise
a business	
	design
a market	
	plan
a product	
	make a profit

2 *PAIRS.* **Which statements do you agree with most? Explain.**

> If you advertise something enough, people will buy it.

> The best ideas are never planned.

> The most successful products are the simplest ones.

> Most people decide to buy a product because of the design of the package.

> The only reason to do business is to make a profit.

Listening

3 🎧 **Listen to the radio program about eBay, an Internet business. Write *T* (true) or *F* (false) after each statement.**

1. Pierre Omidyar started eBay with a vision of a large international company.

2. Products sold on eBay are mainly for collectors.

3. Sellers pay to advertise on eBay.

4. The company doesn't produce its own merchandise.

4 *PAIRS.* **Discuss these questions. Explain your reasons and ask follow-up questions.**

Do you sometimes buy things on the Internet?

What products or services would you *never* get on the Internet?

116

Reading

5 Read the first paragraph of the article. What is Toby Mott's "winning formula"?

A Simple Idea

Toby Mott was just an ordinary person who worked as an artist. But then, at the age of 36, he had an idea that made him famous. It started when he wanted to earn some money for the holidays one year. His product was simple: a short message—five words—on a T-shirt. It was a winning formula.

He took the T-shirts to a clothing store and they sold 40 in a week. Immediately, he decided to start his own business. The product was good; he got the business plan right and it worked. In the past 12 months, he has sold 60,000 T-shirts worldwide.

The phrases for the T-shirts come from things he thinks of during the day and from conversations with friends at dinner. His customers, who include the rich and the famous, enjoy his imaginative phrases. They include things like *I will spend your money*, *I do things I shouldn't*, and *I have nothing to wear*, which he sold to top international model Kate Moss.

Mott says, "I'm successful, but it hasn't changed my personal life. I still work at home on the same small desk, where I produce all the designs. My friends, who I've known for more than 20 years, are still my friends.

"In fact, they're as surprised about my success as I am."

Adapted from *The Sunday Times*

6 Read the whole article. What do these numbers refer to?

5   20   36   40   60,000

7 Read the article again and answer these questions.

1. Why did Toby decide to start his own business?
2. Where does he find new phrases?
3. What do his friends think about him?

Grammar focus

1 Look at the examples of nondefining relative clauses. Underline the relative pronoun in each clause.

> His customers, **who include the rich and the famous**, enjoy his imaginative phrases.
> I still work at home on the same small desk, **where I produce all the designs**.
> eBay, **which has no warehouse, buying, shipping, or returns**, offers no products.
> Pierre, **whose girlfriend was a collector**, created a website.

2 Look at the examples again. Underline the correct words to complete the rules in the chart.

Nondefining relative clauses
A nondefining relative clause adds **essential / extra** information about the preceding noun.
The sentence **will / will not** make sense without the nondefining relative clause.
The relative pronoun *that* **is / is not** used in nondefining relative clauses.
NOTE: Use commas before and after nondefining relative clauses.

Grammar Reference page 149

3 Combine the sentences, using a nondefining relative clause to give the extra information. Add a relative pronoun and make any other changes.

1. TV ads catch most people's attention. The ads are usually very creative.

   TV ads, which are usually very creative, catch most people's attention.

2. Some credit card companies make enormous profits. They often charge high interest rates.

3. My best friend earns a huge salary. She works in advertising.

4. Osaka, Japan, has a spectacular airport. I went there on business last year.

5. Oprah Winfrey is a brilliant businesswoman. She is a famous TV talk-show host.

6. Toby Mott made a lot of money in a short period of time. His business plan was very simple.

7. Many companies market their products to teenagers. Teenagers have a lot of spending power.

8. Mexico City is a shopper's paradise. You can find beautiful and original handmade products there.

9. My friend decided to move to Caracas. He was tired of the cold weather.

10. Australia produces world-famous wool. It has become known as a great wine-producing country.

Pronunciation

4 🎧 Listen. Notice the way the speaker changes intonation and pauses before and after the nondefining relative clause. Then listen again and repeat.

TV ads, which are usually very creative, catch most people's attention.

5 🎧 Listen to the rest of the sentences in Exercise 3. Then practice saying the sentences with a partner.

Speaking

6 *PAIRS.* Imagine that you and your partner want to start a new business. Decide on a product or service. Consider the ideas below or others of your own.

- an Internet company
- a café
- a store
- a delivery company

7 *PAIRS.* Write notes for a business plan. Use the form below.

> Product / Service:
>
> Price:
>
> Advertising / Publicity:
>
> Place:
>
> Other information:

8 *GROUPS OF 4.* Explain your plan to another group.

Our plan is to start a new website for international students. These students, who are eager to make friends from different backgrounds, will be able to find pen pals from other countries. We plan to charge a small fee . . .

Writing

9 Write a letter to a bank manager asking for a loan for a business. Try to include some nondefining relative clauses.

CONVERSATION TO GO

A: I have a business plan, **which I wrote myself**, and the perfect product.

B: Really? Tell me more.

If only . . .

Vocabulary Shopping
Grammar Past unreal conditional; *I wish; If only*
Speaking Talking about regrets

Getting started

1 *PAIRS.* **Use the words and expressions in the box to complete the sentences in the survey.**

bargains	clearance sales	haggling	on impulse	a refund
shop around	take things back	try clothes on	vendors	~~window shopping~~

$4.59

1 Do you go _window shopping_ and look at a lot of things without intending to buy them?

2 Do you ever buy things _____ on your way home from work or school?

3 Do you wait for the _____ at the end of the season, to get _____?

4 Do you _____ in different places to compare prices?

5 How often do you _____ to a store and ask for _____?

6 How do you feel about _____ for a cheaper price?

7 Do you always _____ to see if they fit before buying them?

8 Do you ever buy things from_____ on the street?

2 *PAIRS.* **Take turns asking and answering the questions in Exercise 1.**

Listening

3 🎧 **Listen to two roommates talk about shopping. Answer these questions.**

1. Where did Rita buy the coat?
2. How much did the coat cost at Abbot's?
3. How much did she pay for it?
4. How did Rita feel after she saw the ad?

4 *PAIRS.* **Have you ever bought something and regretted it later? Take turns telling each other about it.**

120

Reading

5 *PAIRS.* **Discuss these questions.**

What kind of things do people buy when they are on vacation?

Do you usually buy souvenirs?

6 **Read the story about Dave and Liz, two tourists in India. Write *T* (true) or *F* (false) after each statement.**

1. The hat seller said the hats cost 300 rupees.
2. Dave realized he had paid too much.
3. Liz didn't think the hat was at all special.
4. Dave was sorry that he bought the hat.
5. Dave decided not to wear the hat again.

Want to buy a hat?

On our first full day in Delhi we went to the Red Fort. A vendor just outside was selling floppy hats. He was wearing a huge pile of them on his head.

"Hello, friend. Want to buy a hat?" he asked.
"How much?" I asked.
"A good price."
"How much?"
"Whatever you like."
"Whatever I like?"
"You name the price."
"How much are they normally?"
"You name the price, friend. Any price—cheap."
"Um . . . 300 rupees*?"

This seemed reasonable to me, but when I said it, he immediately put a hat on my head and waited for me to pay. I'd obviously offered too much, but I didn't really see how I could change my mind, so I gave him the cash.

Liz asked me what I had paid and laughed in my face. I said I didn't care and thought it was a perfectly fair price for what I had bought, because it was a very nice hat. "Haven't you noticed that every other tourist in the city is wearing one?" she said.

I looked around to see if what she had said was true. A group of middle-aged Europeans came out of the fort. More than half of them were wearing my hat.

I wish I hadn't bought the hat now, because I have to wear it all the time just to show Liz that she hadn't influenced me to change my mind.

*300 rupees is about $5 U.S.

Adapted from *Are You Experienced?* by William Sutcliffe

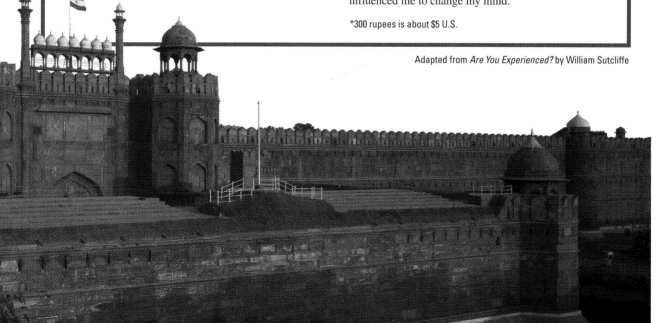

Grammar focus

1   Look at the examples of the past unreal conditional, *I wish*, and *If only*.
Notice the ways to express regret.

> A. **If** I **had known** about the sale, I **would have saved** a lot of money.
> B. **I wish** I hadn't bought the hat.
> C. **If only** I hadn't bought the hat.

2   Look at the examples again and answer these questions.

In example A, did the speaker know about the sale?

In example A, did the speaker save a lot of money?

In examples B and C, did the speaker buy the hat?

3   Look at the examples again. Underline the correct information to complete
the rules in the chart.

> **Past unreal conditional; *I wish*; *If only***
>
> Use the past unreal conditional to talk about **real / imaginary** situations in the past.
>
> In the past unreal conditional, the verb in the *If* clause is in the **simple past / past perfect.**
>
> The verb in the result clause is made of *would* + *have* + the **past participle / base form** of the verb.
>
> Use *I wish I* or *If only I* + the **simple past / past perfect** to express regret about something you did.

> *Grammar Reference page 149*

4   Combine each pair of statements. Use the past unreal conditional, *I wish* or *If only*.
Use each form three times.

1. He didn't haggle with the vendor. He was ripped off.

   He wishes/If only he had haggled with the vendor. OR

   If he had haggled with the vendor, he wouldn't have been ripped off.

2. She bought that skirt on impulse. She wasted her money.

3. I didn't shop around. I got a bad deal.

4. You didn't wait for the sale. You paid too much.

5. We lost the receipt. The store didn't give us a refund.

6. I bought a CD player at a clearance sale. I couldn't
   take it back to the store.

7. I spent all afternoon window shopping. I didn't
   have time to study for my test.

8. Mike didn't try on the suit in the store. The pants
   don't fit him.

9. I bought presents for everyone. My credit card bill
   is huge.

Pronunciation

5 🎧 **Listen.** Notice that the sound /n/ can form a syllable by itself without a vowel sound.

I did**n**'t see the ad.

If I'd seen the ad, I would**n**'t have bought it from a vendor.

I wish I had**n**'t bought the hat.

If I had**n**'t bought the hat, I would**n**'t have felt so stupid!

If only I had**n**'t forgott**en** her birthday.

If I had**n**'t forgott**en** her birthday, she would**n**'t have gott**en** upset.

6 🎧 **Listen again and repeat.**

7 *PAIRS.* Take turns reading the sentences you wrote for Exercise 4.

Speaking

8 *BEFORE YOU SPEAK.* **Complete the notes. Write notes about something that you regret you . . .**

did

didn't do

said

didn't say

9 *GROUPS OF 4.* **Discuss your regrets. Ask and answer follow-up questions.**

A: *I wish I hadn't stayed up until midnight playing video games.*
B: *Why?*
A: *If I hadn't stayed up late, I wouldn't have been so tired, and I would have done better on my exam this morning.*

10 **Share your group's regrets with the rest of the class. Did anyone have similar regrets? Is it true that "you only regret what you did *not* do"?**

Both Akiko and Hisa wish they had traveled to the U.S. and Canada when they had the chance.

Writing

11 **Think about something that someone close to you did that you wish he or she hadn't done. Explain what the person did and describe your feelings about it. Describe how things might have been different if he or she hadn't done it.**

CONVERSATION TO GO

A: That coat doesn't fit you.
B: I know. I wish I hadn't bought it.

27

Lesson A

Positive thinking

Vocabulary Adjectives describing personalities
Grammar Verb + infinitive, verb + gerund, and preposition + gerund
Speaking Talking about future plans and attitudes

Getting started

1 *PAIRS.* **Look at the pictures on page 125. How would you describe the two people? Why?**

2 *PAIRS.* **Look at the adjectives describing personalities. Mark each one, ✓ for positive or X for negative.**

bitter X	level-headed	cheerful	optimistic	cynical
pessimistic	easygoing	short-tempered	glum	sociable

3 *PAIRS.* **Answer each question with an adjective from Exercise 2.**

How would you describe someone who . . .

1. is friendly and enjoys being with other people? *sociable*
2. believes that good things will happen in the future?
3. usually expects bad things to happen?
4. is pleasant and happy?
5. often feels sad?
6. is very angry because of something that happened in the past?
7. gets angry easily?
8. is usually relaxed and doesn't worry?
9. distrusts other people and doesn't believe they have good intentions?
10. is calm and sensible and shows good judgment?

4 *PAIRS.* **Which words in Exercise 2 describe you? Are you the type of person who sees the glass as half empty or half full?**

Listening

5 🎧 **Listen to five people talking. Which adjectives in Exercise 2 describe each of them?**

1. _optimistic_ 2. _____ 3. _____ 4. _____ 5. _____

Reading

6 What are you—an optimist or a pessimist? Complete the questionnaire to find out.

7 *PAIRS.* Count the number of a's, b's, and c's you chose. Then look at the key on page 141. Is the statement about you true? Tell your partner.

Optimist OR Pessimist?

1 How do you see your future?

a. You plan to live to the age of 100, active and full of energy. You can't imagine sitting around all day.

b. You expect to get run over by a bus any day, so why think about living a long life?

c. You look forward to retiring and enjoying a good life. You know you can't help having some problems but hope they won't be serious.

2 Someone you've met at work has invited you to a party. How do you feel?

a. You're excited about going. You're hoping to meet lots of new and interesting people, and have a fabulous evening.

b. You avoid going to parties because you're not very sociable. What's wrong with staying home instead of being bored to tears by strangers?

c. Your new co-worker seems to be friendly enough and you hope to meet at least a few new faces.

3 You've arranged to go on a picnic with friends.

a. You're looking forward to having a wonderful time in perfect weather.

b. You're afraid of getting caught in a rainstorm. You won't leave home without checking the weather forecast several times.

c. You're hoping to have pleasant weather.

4 You have just been invited to a workshop about how positive thinking can influence the rest of your life.

a. You can't imagine having anything negative ever happen to you, but you'll attend anyway.

b. You're not interested in thinking positively when so many terrible things will happen anyway. (And you *don't* think you're cynical, just realistic!)

c. You choose to try it out. You are not convinced it will change your life, but you don't mind adopting a positive outlook and seeing how long it lasts.

Grammar focus

1 Look at the examples of verbs followed by infinitives or gerunds and prepositions followed by gerunds. Label each pair *preposition + gerund, verb + infinitive,* or *verb + gerund*.

_____ You **plan to live** to the age of 100.
Your co-worker **seems to be** friendly.

_____ You **can't imagine sitting** around all day.
You **don't mind adopting** a positive attitude.

_____ You **look forward to retiring**.
You won't leave home **without checking** the weather forecast.

2 Look at the words in the box. Write *I* (infinitive) or *G* (gerund) next to each one, depending on the verb form that goes after each.

Verb + infinitive, verb + gerund, preposition + gerund			
about _G_	afraid of _____	avoid _____	by _____
can't help _____	choose _____	expect _____	hope _____
imagine _____	instead of _____	interested in _____	plan _____
look forward to _____	mind _____	of _____	without _____
seem _____	try _____	think about _____	

Grammar Reference page 150

3 Complete the ad with the correct form of the verbs in parentheses.

MIND POWER SYSTEM

When you get up in the morning, do you . . .
• try **(1)** _to look_ **(look)** on the bright side each day?
• expect **(2)**_____ **(face)** one crisis after another?
• look forward to **(3)**_____ **(be)** in a good mood?
• plan **(4)**_____ **(feel)** pessimistic and glum?
If you're sick and tired of **(5)**_____ **(be)** sick and tired, we have good news for you!

Imagine **(6)**_____ **(think)** positive thoughts all the time. With our proven Mind Power System, you can take control of your life by **(7)**_____ **(change)** your thoughts. This amazing system will work for you without **(8)**_____ **(waste)** hours of your valuable time. Give us 10 minutes a day if you're interested in **(9)**_____ **(get)** more out of your life for the better!

Remember, you can choose
(10) _____ **(change) your life**
for the better!

GUARANTEED!

Pronunciation

4 🎧 **Listen. Notice the words that are stressed. How are the words *to* and *of* pronounced?**

You **plan** to **live** to the **age** of a **hun**dred. You ex**pect** to be **full** of **en**ergy.

You **look for**ward to re**ti**ring. You **hope** to **trav**el and **see lots** of **new plac**es.

You **stay home** instead of **go**ing to the **pic**nic. You're a**fraid** of getting **caught** in the **rain**.

5 🎧 **Listen again and repeat.**

Speaking

6 *GROUPS OF 3.* **Make notes about your hopes, plans, and dreams for the future under "Student A." Then take a survey of your classmates' thoughts about the future. Find out if they are optimistic or pessimistic.**

A: *What do you plan to do in the future?*
B: *I plan to take a long trip to Canada. I look forward to seeing some beautiful scenery and practicing my English, too!*

Thoughts about the future	Student A	Student B	Student C
Plan / hope to do			
Interested in / look forward to doing			
Don't mind doing			

7 **Share with the class anything interesting you discovered about your classmates' hopes and dreams.**

Antonio is interested in studying aerospace engineering. He plans to become an engineer and even hopes to be an astronaut someday.

Writing

8 **Write a letter to a close friend or family member describing your hopes, plans, and dreams for the future. Use some verbs + infinitives and verbs/prepositions + gerunds as appropriate.**

CONVERSATION TO GO

A: If you **need to borrow** money, ask a pessimist.
B: How come?
A: A pessimist **doesn't expect to get** the money back.

Ice maiden

Vocabulary People, traditions, and groups
Grammar Past modals: *may have, might have, could have, can't have,*
must have for past deduction
Speaking Drawing conclusions about the past

Getting started

1 **Match the words with the definitions.**

1. customs ___h___   a. way of doing something that has existed for a long time

2. culture ____   b. social or professional position (in relation to other people)

3. tradition ____   c. the ideas, beliefs, and art common to a group of people

4. tribe ____   d. members of a family or social group of about the same age

5. society ____   e. a family member who lived and died long ago

6. status ____   f. people living together in an organized way with the same laws and similar ways of doing things

7. ancestor ____   g. a group of people of the same race who share beliefs and language, and live in a particular area

8. generation ____   h. practices shared by a group of people

2 *GROUPS OF 3.* **Discuss. Do you know of any customs that your ancestors followed? Do you do the same?**

An Amazing Discovery

Reading

3 *PAIRS.* **Look at the pictures and discuss these questions.**

Who are these people? What are they doing?
What do you think they have discovered?

4 **Read the first paragraph of the article and check your answers.**

5 **Read the rest of the article. Write a reason for each of these facts about the Ice Maiden.**

1. She was very tall. *She had extra food because of her status.*

2. Her blouse was made of fine silk.

3. She wore a very big headdress.

4. She had a hole in her head.

5. She had tattoos of animals on her body.

6 *PAIRS.* **Compare your answers.**

Listening

7 **Listen to two people discuss a TV documentary about the Ice Maiden. Write *T* (true) or *F* (false) after each statement.**

1. The Ice Maiden probably rode horses.
2. Silk was produced by her tribe.
3. The tribe probably traveled outside their own area.
4. The Ice Maiden was definitely a warrior.

In 1993, an amazing discovery was made in the Siberian mountains. A team of archaeologists found a woman who had been buried 2,500 years ago. They called her the Ice Maiden because the ice had preserved her body, her clothes, and her possessions within the burial site. They discovered that she was from the Pazyryk people, a tribe who had once lived there. And by looking at her things, they realized that she must have been someone very special. But who was she? And what was her position in society?

Five foot six The team found that the Ice Maiden was 5 feet 6 inches in height (1.70 meters)—extremely tall for a woman at that time. It is not clear why she was so tall—she might have had extra food because of her status.

Dressed in fine clothing The Ice Maiden wore a blouse made of precious silk, which means she must have been wealthy. And only important people wore tall headdresses—she was wearing a 3-foot-tall headdress. It was covered in gold, which clearly showed she was an important and powerful woman in her family and in her tribe.

Hole in the head The archaeologists found a large hole in the back of her head. This was probably part of a process for preserving important people when they died, a custom of the Pazyryk culture. This young woman can't have been an ordinary member of society.

Fabulous tattoos Her body was covered with fabulous tattoos. The archaeologists now think that she may have been a storyteller. Storytellers were very important members of the Pazyryk society. They memorized the history of their ancestors and used the tattoos of animals to illustrate the stories. In this way, they passed on the beliefs and traditions to future generations. In addition, she could have been a religious figure with the ability to heal or predict the future. Obviously, she had a special position in this culture.

Grammar focus

1 Study the examples of past modals. Notice the ways to express past deduction.

> She **may have been** a storyteller.
> She **might have had** extra food.
> She **might not have been** a warrior.
> She **could have been** a religious figure.
> Silk **can't have come** from the area they lived in.
> The tattoos **must have illustrated** stories that she passed on from her ancestors.

2 Look at the examples again. Complete the rules in the chart with the correct past modals: *may have, might have, could have, can't have,* or *must have*. Then answer the question.

Past modals: *may have, might have, could have, can't have, must have*
I'm almost certain it was true _____
I think it was possible _____ , _____ , _____
I'm almost certain it wasn't true _____
What form of the verb always follows the past modal? _____

> *Grammar Reference page 150*

Grammar Reference page 150

3 Make deductions about the past using the cues and *may have, might have, could have, can't have,* or *must have*. There may be more than one answer.

1. She was very tall for a woman of her time. The reason isn't clear, but she
   <u>may/might/could have received</u> **(receive)** special medical care.

2. She wore a gold headdress. Only wealthy people wore tall headdresses, so she _____ **(be)** rich.

3. She was wearing a silk blouse. We don't know where the silk was from, but it _____ **(come)** from China or India.

4. She remembered long stories, something very difficult to do. She _____ **(have)** a bad memory.

5. The Ice Maiden was found with a mysterious hole in her head. Her tribe _____ **(preserve)** people this way.

6. They buried them with weapons. They _____ **(be)** warriors.

7. She was wearing riding boots. She _____ **(ride)** horses.

8. The tribe had things from distant lands. They _____ **(travel)** to faraway places.

Pronunciation

4 🎧 **Listen. Notice the weak pronunciation of *have* and the way it is linked to the word before it.**

She must h̶ave been someone important.

She could h̶ave been a religious figure.

The silk can't h̶ave come from that area.

She may h̶ave been a storyteller.

She might not h̶ave been a warrior.

It might h̶ave come from China.

5 🎧 **Listen again and repeat.**

Speaking

6 *BEFORE YOU SPEAK.* **Think about what life was like 2,500 years ago. Take notes. Use these ideas or others of your own.**

- entertainment
- families
- farming
- food
- houses
- illness
- religion
- transportation

7 *GROUPS OF 3.* **Discuss your ideas and explain your reasons.**

A: People must have lived much shorter lives because there were no doctors or hospitals.
B: True, but they might have had natural remedies for illnesses.

Writing

8 **Think about a person or time period in the past. Compare that person's life or that time period with life as we know it today. Use past modals for deduction.**

CONVERSATION TO GO

A: Life **must have been** harder 1,000 years ago.
B: Yes, but it **might have been** quieter.

Unit 25 A winning formula

1 Read the ad for a wireless phone. Do you think it is a good product? Why?

We are proud to introduce the LightTouch phone, which sets a new standard in wireless technology. This new model, which is designed to do more than any other wireless device, lets you stay in touch when you're away from your computer.

- *Get on the Internet with the phone's built-in browser, which can also send email.*
- *Send multimedia messages, which may include voice, sound, and pictures.*
- *Snap pictures of all your friends, who can save them on their own computers.*
- *Create your own videos, which you can play over and over with the built-in video player.*

The LightTouch phone, which weighs only 4 ounces, is convenient enough to carry in your pocket.

2 *GROUPS OF 3.* Make up an ad for a product. You can use one of these products or your own idea. Include six selling points. Use at least one nondefining relative clause in your ad.

- a DVD player and recorder
- an athletic shoe
- a new video game

3 *GROUPS OF 3.* Present your product to the rest of the class. Each member of the group gives two selling points.

Unit 26 If only . . .

4 🎧 Listen to a man talk to a friend about his new LightTouch phone. What does the man regret? What does he wish he had done differently?

5 *PAIRS.* Think of a product or service that you have bought or rented that you later regretted. Take turns talking about what happened.

- Explain the background and what you bought or paid for.
- What went wrong? Why?
- What do you wish you had done differently? What would the result have been?

Unit 27 Positive thinking

6 *PAIRS.* Read the situations below. Imagine your reaction to each situation. Take turns being the optimist and the pessimist. What do you think will happen in each situation?

Student A, for 1–3, you are the optimist. For 4–6, you are the pessimist.
Student B, for 1–3, you are the pessimist. For 4–6, you are the optimist.

1. You are a struggling actor/actress. You have an audition for a part in a play tomorrow.
2. Your teacher is about to return midterm tests to the class, with your grades on them.
3. You've decided to buy a new computer. You're not sure where to shop for the best value.
4. Your boss at work has asked you to come into her office. You don't know why.
5. You have applied to a university for admission. You open your mailbox and find a letter from the university.
6. You are on your way to the airport to catch a plane. The weather forecast predicts thunderstorms.

7 Compare your reactions with the rest of the class.

Unit 28 Ice maiden

8 *PAIRS.* Discuss these questions.

What do you know about dinosaurs?
Why do you think they disappeared?

9 🎧 Listen to part of a lecture about what happened to the dinosaurs. Two theories are discussed. Take notes on those two theories.

- giant meteor/explosion
- space aliens took them
- dust blocked the sun
- ice age
- long winter/plants died
- humans killed them

10 *PAIRS.* Use the ideas in the note and others of your own to discuss the reasons why the dinosaurs may have disappeared. Discuss what might or could have happened, what can't have happened, and what must have happened.

World of Music *4*

The Day Before You Came
Abba

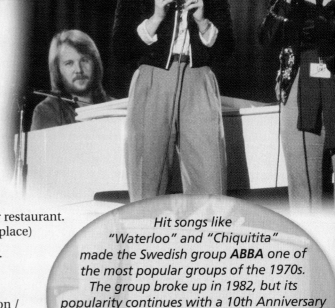

Vocabulary

1 Underline the word or phrase that is similar in meaning to the words in bold in each sentence.

1. My train left the station just when it was **due**.
   (late / supposed to / too early)

2. **Heaps** of paper were waiting to be signed.
   (piles / small amounts / groups)

3. I had lunch with the usual **bunch** at the corner restaurant.
   (amount of food / group of people / particular place)

4. I was **blue** all day yesterday because of the rain.
   (mad / bored / sad)

5. I kept on **dragging** myself to the gym.
   (moving without care / moving without direction / moving without interest)

6. We moved to California with the **aim** of finding a job in the computer industry.
   (love / intensity / goal)

> Hit songs like "Waterloo" and "Chiquitita" made the Swedish group **ABBA** one of the most popular groups of the 1970s. The group broke up in 1982, but its popularity continues with a 10th Anniversary reissue of ABBA Gold and ABBA Oro, the CD that collects ABBA's Spanish language recordings, including the hit "Fernando."

Listening

2 🎧 Listen to the song, but do not look at the lyrics on page 135. What does the singer describe in her song?

a. the day she met someone

b. a special day

c. a typical day in her life

3 🎧 Listen to the song again and complete the lyrics on page 135.

Speaking

4 *GROUPS OF 3.* Discuss these questions. Find the lines in the song that support your ideas.

1. Why does the singer know exactly what she did all day long?

2. How does the singer feel about her life on the day described in the song?

3. Do you think her life changed after that day? In what way?

The Day Before You Came

I must have _____ my house at eight because I always do.

My train, I'm certain, left the station just when it was due.

I must have _____ the morning paper, going into town

And having gotten through the editorial, no doubt I must have _____ .

I must have _____ my desk around a quarter after nine

With letters to be read and heaps of papers waiting to be signed.

I must have _____ to lunch at half past twelve or so,

The usual place, the usual bunch.

And still on top of this I'm pretty sure it must have _____

The day before you came.

I must have _____ my seventh cigarette at half past two

And at the time I never even noticed I was blue.

I must have _____ on dragging through the business of the day

Without really knowing anything I hid a part of me away.

At five I must have _____, there's no exception to the rule.

A matter of routine, I've done it ever since I finished school.

The train back home again undoubtedly I must have _____ the evening paper then.

Oh yes, I'm sure my life was well within its usual frame

The day before you came.

I must have _____ my front door at eight o'clock or so

And stopped along the way to buy some Chinese food to go.

I'm sure I had my dinner watching something on TV.

There's not, I think, a single episode of *Dallas* that I didn't see.

I must have _____ to bed around a quarter after ten.

I need a lot of sleep and so I like to be in bed by then.

I must have _____ a while

The latest one by Marilyn French or something in that style.

It's funny but I had no sense of living without aim

The day before you came.

And turning out the light

I must have _____ and _____ up for yet another night

And rattling on the roof I must have _____ the sound of rain

The day before you came.

Information for pair and group work

Review 1, Exercise 4
Student A

1. **You are a travel agent. Student B will ask you questions about Bangkok, Thailand. Use the information below to answer B's questions.**

The best time for visiting Thailand is between November and February—during these months it doesn't rain so much, and it is not too hot. If you go to Bangkok, the worst two months are April, when it is extremely hot, and October, when it is very wet. Wear lightweight clothes. Casual clothing is fine except when you enter a temple. The Grand Palace, the Temple of the Golden Buddha, and the floating market are popular tourist attractions. You can shop all you want in Bangkok, including the night markets, where you can find inexpensive, good quality clothing and handmade crafts. Thai cooking is delicious, especially if you like spicy foods made with chilies, and you can find an amazing variety of exotic fruits. If you're interested, meditation study is very popular, as well as classes in Thai boxing, Thai cooking, and traditional massage.

2. **Now switch roles. You are the traveler and Student B is the travel agent who will answer your questions. You are planning to take a winter vacation in Colorado, U.S. Find out about:**

- the best months to go
- the weather and snowfall
- winter sports and attractions
- the scenery
- what clothes to bring
- other outdoor activities

Review 1, Exercise 5
Student A

Recipe: Scrambled eggs for two

4 eggs
1/4 cup milk
1 tablespoon butter
salt
ground pepper

In a small bowl, mix together the eggs, milk, and a pinch of salt. In a skillet, melt the butter over medium heat. Pour the egg mixture into the pan, stirring slowly. As the eggs begin to set (become less liquid), turn the heat up to high and shake the pan. Continue cooking and stirring occasionally until the eggs are set. Season with fresh ground pepper and serve.

Unit 16, Exercise 4
Student A

Look at your information and decide what questions you need to ask Student B in order to complete the information about Madonna. Student B will also ask questions.

A: *When was Madonna born?*
B: *In 1958.*

1. Madonna was born in _____ (when) in Bay City, Michigan, U.S.

2. She was named _____ (what) by her parents.

3. Her first recording contract was signed in 1982.

4. Her first big pop music recording, "Holiday," was released in _____ . (when)

5. Madonna's image as a Marilyn Monroe look-alike was introduced in her music video "Material Girl."

6. Her controversial song "Justify My Love" was banned by MTV because _____ . (why)

7. She was awarded a Golden Globe for her portrayal of Eva Peron in the movie *Evita.*

8. Today, the entertainer who is most admired by Madonna is _____ . (who)

Unit 22, Exercise 7
Student A

Ask Student B questions about these situations. First decide if the situation is possible or unlikely, then ask a question starting with:

What would you do if . . . ? OR
What will you do if . . . ?

- Your boss won't let you take a vacation for a year.
- You set up an appointment with an important client, then you remember you have a social appointment at the same time.
- Your best friend asks you for a ride to the airport at 5:00 tomorrow morning.
- You have a lot of homework tonight and you're exhausted.
- (Make up your own situation.)

Now switch roles. Student B will ask you questions, some of them possible, some hypothetical. Answer B's questions starting with:

I will (I'll) OR
I would (I'd)

Unit 7, Exercise 7
Student A

You are the director of Sweet Dreams—a big company that makes chocolates. You are going to have a meeting with a sales representative from a security company (Student B). Explain your problems (in the memo below) and see if he/she has any products that can help you. You have a budget of $20,000 to spend.

Our employees may be making long personal calls because our phone bill went up by 30 percent. Can you help me with this problem?

MEMO

- 30% increase in phone bills. Are employees making long personal calls?

- Two employees were robbed last week leaving work—no lights in the parking lot.

- 10% of chocolates disappear every week in the shipping department—maybe workers are eating them, but no evidence.

- Saw the sales manager playing computer games. How many others do this?

Unit 9, Exercise 6
Student A

Read the forecast. Decide whether you should have the beach party.

On Channel 11, they said that . . .

Channel 11 forecast
Have you noticed the dry air today? It's no surprise because bright sunshine and dry weather are coming in the next few days. This time the popular saying got it right—we expect good weather when there is no "r" in the month. After looking at my computers, I expect there will be warm and sunny conditions for the next few days.

Review 4, Exercise 7
Student A

Look at your information and decide what questions you need to ask Student B in order to complete the information about Venus and Serena Williams. Student B will also ask questions.

1. Venus Williams was born in June 1980.
2. Serena Williams was born in _____ .
3. When the girls were only three years old, they were taught to play tennis by their father, Richard.
4. They are managed and coached by their father.
5. Early in their careers they were called _____ by the press.
6. Venus's serve was recorded at 127 miles per hour—the women's world record.
7. _____ was defeated by Venus in the women's singles final to make Venus the Wimbledon 2001 champion.
8. In 2002 Venus was defeated by her sister Serena, the new Wimbledon champion.
9. _____ was honored as the 2003 Female Athlete of the Year at the annual ESPY awards.

Review 5, Exercise 9
Student B

Play the quiz game. Student A gives the answers first, then you identify *who, which, when, that, where,* or *whose.* Find the right clues below to help you.

- time of the day / begins to get dark then
- author / wrote the Harry Potter books
- state of the U.S. / once called the Sandwich Islands
- martial art / originated in Japan
- famous movie director / made thrillers
- place / beer is made
- sport / started in Scotland
- place in Egypt / you can see the Sphinx and the great pyramids there

Review 1, Exercise 4
Student B

1. You are planning to take a vacation in Bangkok, Thailand. Your partner, Student A, is a travel agent. Find out about:

   - the best (and worst) times to go
   - the weather
   - other interesting things to do
   - what to bring
   - sight-seeing
   - the shopping

2. Now switch roles. You are a travel agent. Student A will ask you questions about Colorado, U.S. Use the information below to answer A's questions.

Colorado is a magnificent place for a winter vacation, with some of the best skiing, snowmobiling, and snowboarding in North America. The mountain resorts get about 300 inches of snow a year, and it snows *somewhere* each month except August. Snowfall arrives early and stays late: many resorts are open from mid-October until June. There are ski slopes for every level, from expert to beginner, so it's perfect if you're taking the family. Bring your warm ski clothes and don't forget the sunblock if you don't want to get burned.

Love beautiful scenery but hate crowds? There are delightful mountain trails for hiking and camping, especially from June through October. Be sure to bring good hiking boots, insect repellent, and warm clothes for nighttime, when it can get pretty cool. Rocky Mountain National Park, sometimes called "America's Switzerland," has spectacular high-mountain landscapes. If you'd like to view wildlife such as deer, elk, and bighorn sheep, the best time is in late September and early October.

Review 1, Exercise 5
Student B

Recipe: Basic bean soup

1 pound dry beans	In a large bowl, combine the beans with the water. Cover and let them soak overnight.
8 cups water	
12 baby carrots	In a large pot, over medium to high heat, combine the soaked beans with water, carrots, onion, and ham. Add more water to cover all the ingredients, if necessary. Bring to a boil, then reduce heat to low and simmer for 4 to 6 hours. Season with salt and pepper to taste and serve.
1 cup chopped onion	
1/2 pound chopped ham	
salt and pepper to taste	

Unit 9, Exercise 6
Student B

Read the forecast. Decide whether you should have the beach party.

On Channel 12, they said that . . .

Channel 12 forecast

There's a saying that goes:

   If salt is sticky and gains in weight,
   it will rain before too late.

Well, for us today the picture is that a tropical storm from the south will bring hot and humid weather for the next couple of days. We will have scattered showers, especially in the morning. The temperature will remain high throughout the area.

Unit 16, Exercise 4
Student B

Look at your information and decide what questions you need to ask Student A in order to complete the information about Madonna. Student A will also ask questions.

A: When was Madonna born?
B: In 1958.

1. Madonna was born in 1958 in _____ . (where)
2. She was named Madonna Louis Veronica Ciccone by her parents.
3. Her first recording contract was signed in _____ . (when)
4. Her first big pop music recording, "Holiday," was released in 1983.
5. Madonna's image as a Marilyn Monroe look-alike was introduced _____ . (where)
6. Her controversial song "Justify My Love" was banned by MTV because it was considered too shocking.
7. She was awarded a Golden Globe for _____ . (what/for)
8. Today, the entertainer who is most admired by Madonna is Britney Spears.

Unit 5, Exercise 7
Student A

In each situation, the person underlined refers to your partner (Student B). Ask Student B for permission.

A: Can I use your computer?
B: I'm sorry, but I need it to do my homework.

1. Your computer isn't working and you want to check your email. <u>Your roommate</u> has a computer.

2. You're in a café. There are four of you, but there are only three chairs around the table. <u>The person at the next table</u> is alone and there are extra chairs around his/her table.

3. A friend is coming to visit you and is bringing a lot of luggage. <u>Your sister/brother</u> has a car. You want to borrow it so you can meet your friend at the airport.

4. You're on a train. The window is open and you're cold. There's <u>a stranger</u> sitting across from you.

Unit 5, Exercise 8
Student A

Listen to your partner. Use the cues to respond to Student B.

1. Give permission.
2. Refuse permission because you're trying to study.
3. Give permission.
4. Refuse permission because you left it at home.

Review 3, Exercise 7
Student A

You are the manager of an electronics superstore. You are looking for a new salesperson. Find out the following information from the person you interview:

- [ ] past experience/responsibilities
- [ ] reason(s) for leaving previous job(s)
- [ ] experience in sales
- [ ] knowledge of electronics
- [ ] can work nights/weekends
- [ ] strengths/weaknesses

Review 4, Exercise 7
Student B

Look at your information and decide what questions you need to ask Student A in order to complete the information about Venus and Serena Williams. Student A will also ask questions.

1. Venus Williams was born in June _____ .

2. Serena Williams was born in September 1981.

3. When the girls were only _____ years old they were taught to play tennis by their father, Richard.

4. They are managed and coached by _____ .

5. Early in their careers they were called "Slice Girls" and "Sister Act" by the press.

6. Venus's serve was recorded at _____ miles per hour—the women's world record.

7. Justine Henin was defeated by Venus in the women's singles final to make Venus the Wimbledon 2001 champion.

8. In 2002 Venus was defeated by _____ , the new Wimbledon champion.

9. Serena was honored as the 2003 Female Athlete of the Year at the annual ESPY awards.

Review 5, Exercise 10
Student A

Now Student B gives the answers first, then you identify *who, which, when, that, where,* or *whose.* Find the right clues below to help you.

- master of Kung Fu / became a movie actor
- great Spanish artist / invented cubism
- sports / started in the U.S.
- boy / his nose grew longer whenever he told a lie
- name of currency / used in Canada and the U.S.
- place / you buy medicine there
- time / the day and night are the same length
- Chinese philosopher / started the religion of Confucianism

Information for pair and group work

Unit 9, Exercise 6
Student C

Read the forecast. Decide whether you should have the beach party.

On Channel 13, they said that . . .

Channel 13 forecast
The satellite shows a very variable picture. The heavy rain that has been affecting the southern part of the country will be with us tomorrow. Many areas can expect winds and light showers. There will be a chance of fog—maybe even dense fog—in some areas. However, there are signs of good weather on the way.

Review 3, Exercise 7
Student B

You are interviewing for a job as a salesperson in an electronics superstore. Your partner (Student A), who is the store manager, will ask you questions. Use the following, in addition to your own information, to answer the questions:

Your last job was as a salesperson in a clothing store.
You left because the store went out of business.
You've had a few sales jobs as a student in the summer.
You love electronics; you have all the latest gadgets.
You can work nights but won't be able to work weekends.
You're responsible and creative, but not organized.

Review 5, Exercise 9
Student A

Play the quiz game. You give the answers first, then Student B identifies *who, which, when, that, where,* or *whose*.

Alfred Hitchcock	Giza	Judo
a brewery	Hawaii	golf
dusk	J. K. Rowling	

Review 5, Exercise 10
Student B

Now you give the answers first, then Student A identifies *who, which, when, that, where,* or *whose*.

Bruce Lee	the equinox	the dollar
Confucius	Pablo Picasso	Pinocchio
a pharmacy	basketball, baseball, and volleyball	

Unit 22, Exercise 7
Student B

Student A will ask you questions, some of them possible, some hypothetical. Answer A's questions starting with:

I will (I'll) OR
I would (I'd)

Now switch roles. Ask Student A questions about these situations. First decide if the situation is possible or unlikely, then ask a question starting with:

What would you do if . . . ? OR
What will you do if . . . ?

- You're in a meeting conducted in English and you don't understand everything.
- You have a job that you like, and another company offers you a better job.
- You're in an important meeting (or in class) and your cell phone rings because you forgot to turn it off.
- You are invited to dinner as a guest and they serve a food that you're allergic to.
- (Make up your own situation.)

Unit 5, Exercise 3
Students A and B

1. T
2. F
3. T (Even when invited, people may offer to pay for their meal, though no one expects the offer to be taken.)
4. T
5. T (It's OK to arrive up to 15 minutes late. As a general rule, guests shouldn't arrive early.)
6. F (You should ask permission first.)
7. F (Try to make eye contact with the server to get his/her attention.)
8. F
9. T
10. T (In fact, in most public places in the U.S., smoking isn't allowed at all.)
11. F
12. F

Unit 5, Exercise 7
Student B

Listen to your partner. Use the cues to respond to Student A.

A: Can I use your computer?
B: I'm sorry, but I need it to do homework.

1. Refuse permission because you need it to do homework.

2. Refuse permission because you're waiting for some friends.

3. Refuse permission because you need it to get to work.

4. Give permission.

Unit 5, Exercise 8
Student B

In each situation, the person underlined refers to your partner (Student A). Ask Student A for permission.

1. You are going to your friend's party, and you would like to stay overnight because the last train home is at 11 P.M.

2. You want to watch television. Your roommate is reading.

3. You need to leave class early because you have a doctor's appointment. Your teacher is very strict.

4. You are in an English class and you need a dictionary. You think your classmate has one.

Unit 27, Exercise 7
Students A and B

KEY: If you chose mostly . . .

a's: Lucky you! You are very cheerful and always look on the bright side of life! The future looks good.

b's: Cheer up and stop being so glum. Things aren't as bad as you think. Try to change your outlook a little.

c's: You are very level-headed and logical. There won't be any surprises for you tomorrow.

Unit 7, Exercise 7
Student B

You are a sales representative from Safe & Sound, a security company. Your products are listed below. You are going to have a meeting with the director of a chocolate company (Student A). First, find out his/her needs. Then try to sell your products. Remember to explain what the devices can do and what they can prevent.

A: Our employees may be making long personal calls because our phone bill went up by 30 per cent. Can you help me with this problem?
B: Yes, we can. We have something called "Call Stopper," which many companies use to stop long phone calls.

Safe & Sound
Product List

- "Light Up"—a security light that comes on when it senses movement. **$1000**

- "Call Stopper"—a device that stops telephone calls to "unauthorized" numbers. **$600**

- "Micro Cam"—a tiny (2 in × 2 in) video camera. **$500**

- "Stop IT Now!"—latest technology to prevent computer users from using certain kinds of software (such as games). **$400**

Unit 9, Exercise 7
Students A, B, and C

There was a mixture of sun and rain yesterday. The result was dense fog, which covered the region for 24 hours. Driving conditions were extremely dangerous and people were advised to stay home. The temperatures were low. But better weather is expected next week.

Grammar reference

Unit 1

Present perfect with *yet, already, just*

- Use the present perfect to talk about things that happened in the past and have an effect on the present.
  *My neighbor **has** just **painted** his front door.*
  (It looks good now.)
  *Kim **has** already **written** her report.*
  (The report is finished now.)

- Use **not yet** when something has not happened but you expect it to happen or be completed in the future.
  *George hasn't finished that book **yet**.*
  (But he'll finish it in a few days.)

- Use **just** when the action happened very recently.
  *I've **just** washed the car.*
  (I finished washing it a few minutes ago.)

- Use **already** when the action is completed sooner than expected.
  *I've **already** cleaned up my desk.*
  (My desk is neat and clean now.)

- Use **yet** to ask whether something has happened that you are expecting will happen. **Yet** is used in questions and negative sentences.
  *Have you done your homework **yet**?*
  (Is your homework finished?)
  *I haven't finished **yet**.*

- **Just** goes between *have* and the past participle.
  *He has **just** cleaned the house.*

- **Yet** usually goes at the end of a clause.
  *I haven't walked the dog **yet**.*

- **Already** goes either between *have* and the past participle or at the end of the clause.
  *She has **already** bought some plants.*
  *She has bought some plants **already**.*

Note: You may also use the past tense with **yet**, **already**, and **just**.
*Did you eat **yet**?*
*I **already** ate.*
*I **just** had breakfast.*

Unit 2

Real conditional

- Use the real conditional to talk about future possibilities.
  ***Will** I **need** rain gear **if** I **go** in June?*

- Use the real conditional to make suggestions and to give advice or warnings.
  *If you **plan** several flights, it **will be** cheaper to buy a pass.*
  *If you **book** your flight well in advance, you **may get** a better price.*
  *If you **use** sunscreen, you **won't get** sunburned.*

- The **if** clause states the condition (what needs to happen).
  *If I **have the time**, I'll help you with your homework.*
  (I will help you under the condition that I have time.)

- Use the simple present in the **if** clause and the future with *will* or *be going to*, a modal, or the imperative in the **result clause**.

If clause (condition): Simple present	Result clause: Future or imperative
If you **go** to Australia,	you**'ll see** beautiful landscapes.
	are you **going to bring** me a souvenir?
	I **can lend** you a travel guide.
	take me with you.

- **Unless** means **if not**.
  *Don't go to Australia **unless** you like hot weather.*
  (Don't go to Australia **if** you **don't** like hot weather.)

Note: The **if** clause can go before or after the result clause. Use a comma to separate the two clauses *only* when the **if clause** begins the sentence.
*If you **use** sunscreen, you **won't get** sunburned.*
*You **won't get** sunburned **if** you **use** sunscreen.*

Unit 3

Count/non-count nouns and quantifiers

- Use these quantifiers with count nouns: ***a few, a number of, each, few, (not) many, several***.
  *We need **a few** onions and **several** cloves of garlic.*

- Use these quantifiers with non-count nouns: ***a little, a great deal of, a little bit of, much, plenty of***.
  *Use a **little oil**. Don't add too **much flour**.*

- Use these quantifiers with both count and non-count nouns: ***all, a lot of, some, any, most of***.
  *Use almost **all the butter** and **all the potatoes**. Mix in **some onions** and **some salt**.*

Note: Use **few** (with count nouns) and **little** (with non-count nouns) to emphasize a lack of something. **A few** and **a little** mean a small quantity, but have a more positive tone.
*There are **few** good restaurants around here.*
(There aren't many good restaurants here—we need more.)
*There are **a few** good restaurants around here.*
(There are some good restaurants—we have a choice.)

Unit 4

Modals to talk about prediction and speculation

- Use **will** to talk about things that you think are very likely to happen in the future.
  *I'm sure interactive books **will** become very popular.*
  *People **won't** live on other planets.*
  ***Will** we still use cars?*

- Use **may**, **might**, or **could** to talk about possibilities in the future.
  *I think we **may** communicate entirely by email.*
  *We **might not** need telephones at all.*
  *Robots **could** be in every home in 50 years.*

- Use the **base form** of the verb (infinitive without *to*) after *will*, *may*, *might*, and *could*.
  *We will/may/might/could **win** the game tomorrow.*

Note: For some speakers, *may* expresses a higher probability than *might*.

Unit 5

Modals: *may, can, could*, and *Is it OK if . . . ?/Do you mind if . . . ?/Would you mind if . . . ?* for permission

- Use **may**, **can**, and **could** to ask for permission to do something.
***Can** I borrow your car?*	*No, I'm sorry. I need it.*
***Could** I use your cell phone?*	*Sure. Go ahead.*
***May** I leave early today?*	*Of course. / Sure.*

- Use the **base form** of the verb after *may*, *can*, and *could*.
  *May/Can/Could I **be** excused?*

- Use the **simple present** after *Is it OK if* + subject or *Do you mind if* + subject.
  *Is it OK/Do you mind if she **leaves** early today?*

- Use the **simple past form of the verb** after *Would you mind if* + subject.
  *Would you mind if she **left** early today?*

- The affirmative response to ***Do you mind if . . . ? / Would you mind if . . . ?*** is ***No, I don't*** or ***No, I don't mind***. (It means "It's OK.")
  A: Would you mind if she left early today?
  *B: **No**, not at all.* (Meaning she has permission to leave early)

- Use ***Is it OK if . . . ?*** to ask permission in informal situations.
  A: Is it OK if I turn on the TV?
  B: Yes, of course.

Note: *May* is more formal than *could*; *could* is more formal than *can*.

Unit 6

Present perfect and present perfect continuous

- Use both the present perfect and the present perfect continuous to talk about recent actions and situations that have a result in the present.

- Use the present perfect when you focus on the result of a completed activity in the indefinite past.
  *He's **tested** the power device and it works.*
  *I **haven't studied** for my exam—I think I'm going to fail.*
  ***Have** you ever **run** a marathon?*

- Use the present perfect continuous when you focus on an activity that may or may not be completed.
  *He's **been testing** the power device.*
  *I **haven't been studying**; I've been sleeping!*
  ***Have** you **been running**?*

- Use **have/has** + **the past participle** to form the present perfect.
  *I **have seen** this movie before.*
  *She **has been** to my house several times.*

- Use **have/has** + **been** + **gerund** (verb + *ing*) to form the present perfect continuous.
  *I've **been playing** soccer for several years.*

- There are certain verbs that you can use in the present perfect but not usually in the present perfect continuous.
  *We've **known** each other since childhood.*
  *I know her face, but I've **forgotten** her name.*
  *How long **have** you **had** that car?*

Unit 7

Expressions of purpose

- Use expressions of purpose (***to, in order to, so that***, etc.) to give reasons for an action.
  *Security companies are installing cameras **in order to** watch employees.*
  *Software is used **so that** they can record the websites you visit.*

Note the different forms:

to + **verb**
*They use cameras **to spy** on people.*

in order to + **verb**
*They use cameras **in order to spy** on people.*

so that + **subject** + **verb**
*They use cameras **so that they can spy** on people.*

in case + **subject** + **verb**
*They use cameras **in case someone steals** from the store.*

for + **verb** + ***-ing***
*They use cameras **for spying** on people.*

Unit 8
Past perfect

- Use the **past perfect** to talk about an action that happened before another action in the past.
  *When I arrived at the terminal, the plane **had already taken off**.*
  (First the plane took off, then I arrived at the terminal.)

- Form the past perfect with **had + the past participle**.
  *The plane **had left** when I arrived at the airport.*

- *Already* can go between *had* and the past participle or at the end of the sentence, for emphasis.
  *He'd **already** checked out of the hotel.*
  *He'd checked out of the hotel **already**.*

- Use time expressions, such as *by the time*, with the clause in the past tense when the other clause is in the past perfect.
  ***By the time** he **reached** the gate, his plane **had already left**.*

Note: There is a difference between the **past perfect** and the **simple past**.
When I **arrived** at the bus stop, the bus **left**.
(I arrived, and the bus left very soon afterward.)
When I **arrived** at the bus stop, the bus **had left**.
(The bus left; then I arrived.)

Unit 9
Indirect statements

- You can start indirect statements in two ways.
  1. **Subject + *told* + object (+ *that*)**
     ***I told him that** I was ready to go.*
  2. **Subject + *said* (+ *that*)**
     ***I said that** I was ready to go.*

- When you report what somebody said, the verb tenses usually change.
  Simple present—simple past:
  "I'm ready to go."
  *He said that he **was** ready to go.*
  Simple past—past perfect:
  *"We **went** to the movies."*
  *They said they'**d gone** to the movies.*
  Present perfect—past perfect:
  *"I'**ve been** on vacation."*
  *She said she'**d been** on vacation.*

Note: There is no change with the past perfect.
*"Anne **had arrived** late, as usual."*
*He said Anne **had arrived** late, as usual.*

- The time expressions (*yesterday, this week*, etc.) often change with indirect statements.
  *"I saw John **yesterday**."*
  *She said that she had seen John **the day before**.*

- Possessive adjectives and pronouns usually change.
  *"**You** can use **my** dictionary."*
  *He said **I** could use **his** dictionary.*

Note: After *say* and *tell*, you don't need *that*.
Sang-Woo said that he was coming. OR
Sang-Woo said he was coming.
Sang-Woo told me that he was coming. OR
Sang-Woo told me he was coming.

Unit 10
Simple future and future perfect

- Use ***will/won't* + the base form** to say what you think will happen **at some point** in the future (simple future).
  *I think we **will wear** tiny computers on our wrists.*

- Use ***will/won't* + *have* + the past participle** to say that you think something will happen before a point in the future (future perfect).
  *By the year 2150, scientists **will have perfected** the "brainlink" computer.*

Unit 11
Indirect questions

- When you report questions that someone else has asked, the two types of questions are reported in different ways.

  1. **Wh- questions (*who, what, where*, etc.)**
     Subject + *asked (me)* + question word + subject + (modal verb) + main verb

     "What's your date of birth?"
     She asked me what my date of birth was.

- Do not use question word order in the indirect question.
  X She asked me what was my date of birth.

  2. ***Yes/No* questions:**
     Subject + *asked (me)* + *if* or *whether* + subject + (modal verb) + main verb

     "Can you work under pressure?"
     He asked me if I could work under pressure.

Note: With most indirect questions, *if* and *whether* usually mean the same thing. In other constructions (such as conditionals) they are not interchangeable.

- With indirect questions, the verb tenses usually change.
  "Do you like office work?"
  *He asked me whether I **liked** office work.*
  "Have you finished your work?"
  *He asked me if I **had finished** my work.*

Note: For more information about changes of tense in indirect statements, see Unit 9, page 144.

Unit 12

Narrative past tenses: simple past, past continuous, past perfect, past perfect continuous

- Use the past continuous:

  to describe longer actions and events in the past.
  *We **were working** last Monday.*

  to set the scene in a story.
  *The sun **was shining** and a breeze **was blowing** gently across the fields.*

  to talk about an action that was still going on when something else happened.
  *They **were waiting** in line when they saw each other for the first time.*

- Use the simple past to talk about completed activities in the past, often with a time reference (*yesterday, last year,* etc.)
  *Irene and Stella **grew up** on the same street.*
  *They **lived** there from 1990 to 1996.*

- Use the past perfect to talk about an activity that happened before another one in the past.
  *Mary dialed the wrong number because she **had written** it down incorrectly.*

- Use the past perfect continuous to talk about an activity that had been in progress before another one in the past.
  *The ground was wet. It **had been raining**.*

Unit 13

Present unreal conditional

- The form of the present unreal conditional is:
  If + **subject** + **simple past tense form**, **subject** + *would* (or *could* or *might*) + **base form of the verb**

- Use the present unreal conditional to talk about unlikely or imaginary situations in the present and the future.
  *If I **had** a car, I **wouldn't take** the train every day.*
  (But I don't have a car, so I take the train.)
  *Would you stop working **if you won** the lottery?*
  (You probably won't win the lottery.)

- Use *might* or *could* instead of *would* when you are less certain.
  *If I **had** a lot of money, I **might** buy a boat.*

Note: Use *were* instead of *was* with all subjects, both singular and plural (*I, you, he, she, it, we, they*).
*If I **were** rich, I'**d buy** a house abroad.*
*If she **were** taller, she **could be** a model.*

Note: The *if* clause often goes first, but it can go second. When the *if* clause goes first, put a comma after it.
If I were rich, I'd be happier.
I'd be happier if I were rich.

Unit 14

Connectors: *although, despite (not), however, in spite of*

- Use *although*, *despite (not)*, *in spite of*, and *however* to introduce contrasting ideas.
  *Carolina didn't call Peter **although** she'd planned to.*
  ***Despite** going to bed very late, we got up at 6:00.*

- Note the different forms:

  despite or *in spite of* + **noun** or **gerund**
  Despite an early departure, we arrived late.
  Despite leaving early, we arrived late.

  In spite of his health, he climbed the mountain.
  He climbed the mountain, in spite of being in bad health.

  despite not + **gerund**
  Despite not having an alarm clock, I manage to wake up early.

  however + **independent clause**
  *I often work long hours. **However**, I enjoy the job.*

  although + **dependent clause** (subject + verb)
  Although I hate commuting, I love my job.

- Punctuation: dependent clauses or phrases starting with *although*, *despite*, *in spite of* at the beginning of a sentence use a comma to separate the two parts of the sentence. When the dependent clause comes at the end of the sentence, a comma is usually not needed.

  Although I like my job, I don't like commuting.
  I don't like commuting although I like my job.
  When *however* comes at the beginning of a sentence, a comma is often used.
  *I like my job. **However**, I don't like commuting.*

Grammar reference

Unit 15

Tag questions

- Use tag questions to check information or to ask someone to agree with you.
  *The exhibition doesn't end until next week, **does it**?*
  *The movie was great, **wasn't it**?*

- The verb tense in the first part of the sentence and in the tag question is the same.
  *You **finished** all your homework, **didn't you**?*

- To form tag questions:
  If the first part of the sentence is affirmative, the tag is negative.
  *It's a beautiful painting, **isn't it**?*
  If the first part of the sentence is negative, the tag is affirmative.
  *The exhibition doesn't close at lunchtime, **does it**?*

  If the main part of the sentence contains an auxiliary verb or the verb *be*, repeat it in the tag.
  *He hasn't read the book yet, **has** he?*
  *You can ride a bike, **can't you**?*
  *She'd like to get a new job, **wouldn't she**?*
  *We're ready to go, **aren't we**?*

  If the main part of the sentence does not contain an auxiliary or the verb *be*, use *do*, *does*, or *did* in the tag:
  *You finish work at five, **don't you**?*
  *Jun speaks several languages, **doesn't he**?*
  *Maria made all the food herself, **didn't she**?*

- After an affirmative imperative in the main part of the sentence, use *will*, *would*, or *could* in the tag.
  *Pass me the dictionary, **will you**?*
  *Help me carry these boxes, **would you**?*

- The answers to tag questions are as follows.
  *You stayed out late, **didn't you**?*
  Yes. *(= Yes, I stayed out late.)*
  No. *(= No, I didn't stay out late.)*

Note: When the tag question is a real question (checking information), and you are not sure of the answer, use rising intonation:

*The museum is open today, **isn't it**?* ↗

When you know the answer and are just asking for agreement, use falling intonation:

*The stores are crowded today, **aren't they**?* ↘

Unit 16

Passive constructions

- Use the passive when
  you don't know who does the action, OR
  you are not interested in who does the action, OR
  it isn't important who does the action, OR
  you don't want to say who does the action.
  *The winner of the competition **was announced** during the show.*
  (It isn't important who announced the winner.)

- Use the passive in more formal contexts.
  *The new President **was taken** to the White House, where he **was interviewed** by reporters.*

- Use *by* + **agent** (the person or thing) to say who did the action.
  *He was interviewed **by reporters from all over the world**.*
  *The movie was directed **by Almodóvar**.*

Note: The object of an active sentence becomes the subject of the passive sentence. The subject of passive constructions is not the person or thing that does the action.

*People broadcast **the programs**.* (active)
***The programs** are broadcast.* (passive)

- To form the passive, use the verb *be* + **the past participle**.
  *The Spice Girls **were created** by a businessman.*
  *The bridge **is being built** at the moment.*
  *This room **has been painted** recently.*

Unit 17

Verbs followed by infinitive or gerund

- **Use the infinitive after certain verbs and verb phrases,** such as *want, decide, need, learn, promise, would like, would love, would hate, plan, afford, manage, offer*.
  *I **want to eat out** tonight.*
  *Do you **need to buy** some new jeans?*
  *He didn't **promise to write**, but I'm sure he will.*

Note: You can also use **verb + object + infinitive** after the verbs ***want*** and ***would like/love/hate***.

*We'**d love you to come** on vacation with us.*
*They **wanted her to join** the swimming club.*

- **Use the gerund after certain verbs and verb phrases,** such as *like, enjoy, love, hate, finish, go, stop, avoid, spend time, waste time* and **after two-part phrasal verbs** such as *give up, take up, keep on*.
  *I **avoid doing** exercise.*
  *He **keeps on laughing** at me.*
  *Do you **enjoy writing** letters?*
  *I don't **waste time surfing** the Internet.*

Unit 18

Requirement, permission, and prohibition.

- Use **make** to talk about requirement.
  The boss made Peter work late. (Someone forced him to work late.)

- Use **not make** to talk about choice.
  They didn't make her work very hard. (No one forced her to work hard, but she could choose to.)

- Use **let** or **be allowed to** to say that something was permitted.
  Mom let him watch TV every night. (She gave him permission to do this.)
  She was allowed to go dancing on weekends. (Someone gave her permission to do this.)
  Did she let him eat sweets? (Did she give him permission to eat them?)

- Use **not let** or **not be allowed to** to say that something wasn't permitted.
  Her parents didn't let her go dancing on weekends. (They refused her permission to do this.)
  He wasn't allowed to eat sweets. (Someone refused him permission to do this.)

- **Let** and **make** are followed by an object and the base form of the verb.
  They let me do it.
  They didn't make him work.

- You can also use **have to** and **get** to talk about things that are required.
  I had to study all weekend.
  My mother got me to study for the test.

Unit 19

Past perfect and past perfect continuous
(See also Unit 8.)

- Use the past perfect to talk about an action or event that happened before another action in the past.
  When she returned to the U.K., she had already written part of the first book. (First she wrote part of the book; then she returned to the U.K.)

- Use the past perfect continuous to talk about longer activities or situations that happened before another action or event in the past.
  Before 1996, Joanne had been living in Portugal. (Up to 1996, Joanne was living in Portugal.)

- Both the simple past perfect and the past perfect continuous can be used with **for** and **since**. Sometimes the two tenses are interchangeable and have almost the same meaning.
  He had lived in his house for five years before he met his neighbors.
  He had been living in his house for five years before he met his neighbors.
  She had worked at the company since she was 21.
  She had been working at the company since she was 21.

- There are certain verbs that you can use in the past perfect but not *usually* in the past perfect continuous.
  We'd known each other for years before we started dating.
  How long had you owned that car when you finally sold it?
  Our home was burglarized because we had forgotten to lock the windows.

Unit 20

Defining relative clauses

- Use relative pronouns (**that, when, where, which, who, whose**) to introduce relative clauses.
  Lavender has a smell that calms people down.
  I know a place where we can get a good meal.

- Use **who** or **that** for people, **that** or **which** for things, **where** for places, **when** or **that** for times, and **whose** for people and their possessions.
  Jane is the one who told me to buy some lavender oil.
  Lemon has a smell which increases people's energy.
  This is the town where my husband grew up.
  I like the night. It's the time when the town is nice and quiet.
  That was the day that we visited you.
  That's the family whose house we stayed in last summer.

- Use relative clauses to define the person or thing you are talking about.
  That's the man.
  That's the man who bought my house.
  (The relative clause defines "the man.")

- In formal situations **whom** may be used instead of **who** when the pronoun is the object of the clause.
  That's the man.
  That's the man whom I met yesterday.

Note: You can omit the relative pronoun when it is the object in a relative clause.

Cherries are the fruit (that) I like most.

Unit 21

Indefinite pronouns

- Use indefinite pronouns to refer to people and things without naming them.
  Form indefinite pronouns with **any-**, **every-**, **some-**, and **no-**.
  *Is there **anything** I can do?*
  *I think **everybody** is here.*
  *I smell **something** burning.*
  ***No one** said a word.*

- When an indefinite pronoun is the subject, it takes a singular verb.
  ***No one knows** the answer.*
  ***Everyone has been** very kind.*
  ***Something is** going on, but I don't know what it is.*
  ***Is anything** wrong?*

- Use singular pronouns and possessive adjectives with indefinite pronouns.
  ***Everybody** says **he** or **she** is a smart shopper.*
  ***Everyone** likes **his** or **her** town.*

- Use indefinite pronouns starting with **some-** to make an offer.
  *Would you like **something** to eat?*

- Use indefinite pronouns with **any-** in negative sentences and questions.
  *I didn't think **anyone** was still awake at this hour.*
  *Is there **anything** you'd like to say?*

- Use indefinite pronouns starting with **any-** to mean *it doesn't matter which one.*
  *What shall we have for dinner? **Anything** you like.*

- Use indefinite pronouns with **any-** after *if*.
  ***If anyone** calls, please take a message.*
  ***If** there's **anything** I can do to help, just let me know.*

Unit 22

Future real conditional and present unreal conditional
(See also Units 2 and 13.)

- Use the future real conditional to talk about things that will possibly happen under certain conditions.
  ***If** you **have** a business lunch in a Latin American country, it **will be** more leisurely and relaxed.*
  (You may or may not have a business lunch in a Latin American country.)
  ***If** it's sunny tomorrow, I'**ll go** out.*
  (It's possible that it'll be sunny.)

- Use the present unreal conditional to talk about hypothetical, unlikely, or imaginary situations.
  ***If** I **weren't** at a meeting, I'**d be** at home.*
  (But I am at a meeting, so I'm not at home.)

- Use the simple present in the *if* clause and *will* or *going to* + the base form of the verb in the result clause of future real conditional sentences.
  ***If** I **have** time, I'**ll help** you with your homework.*

- Use the past tense form in the *if* clause and *would* + the base form of the verb in the result clause of present unreal conditional sentences.
  ***If** you **kept** an executive waiting, it **would be** an insult.*

Unit 23

Separable and inseparable phrasal verbs

- Phrasal verbs are very common in spoken English. They consist of a verb plus one or two particles, which together have a special meaning.
  *Please **turn off** the lights before you leave.*
  *I was **cleaning out** the closet when I **came across** this old hat.*
  *Do you **get along with** your co-workers?*
  *How do you **put up with** such terrible working conditions?*

- With inseparable phrasal verbs that are transitive (i.e., can take an object), the direct object must go after the particle.
  *I used to **pick on** my younger brother.*
  X *I used to pick my younger brother on.*
  *We left a tip for the server who **waited on** us.*
  X *We left a tip for the server who waited us on.*

- With separable phrasal verbs, a noun or noun phrase can go between the verb and the particle or after the particle.
  *We **gave away** all our old clothes.*
  *We **gave** all our old clothes **away**.*
  *I **handed in** my homework.*
  *I **handed** my homework **in**.*

- With separable phrasal verbs, a pronoun must go between the verb and the particle.
  *We've had some problems, but we've always **worked them out**.*
  X *We've worked out them.*
  *She **called** me **up** last night.*
  X *She called up me last night.*

- Some phrasal verbs are intransitive (i.e., they don't have an object).
  *Unfortunately, our plans **fell through**.*
  *In the end, everything **worked out** just fine.*

Unit 24

Passive causatives and reflexive pronouns

- Form the passive causative with **have** + **object** + **the past participle**.
  *I **had my bike repaired** at the Spokes Shop.*
  *I'm going to **have this room painted**.*

- Use the passive causative to say that someone does something for you.
  I have my hair cut once a month.
  (Someone cuts it for me. I don't cut it.)

- If you want to say who does the action for you, use **by** + **person/thing**.
  *I have my car serviced **by Hot Wheels**.*
  *John has his hair cut **by a friend**.*

- Use reflexive pronouns (**myself, yourself, ourselves**, etc.) to give the subject of the sentence greater emphasis.
  *I do everything **myself**.* (Nobody helps me.)
  *When Peter was little, he never did anything **himself**. His mother did it all.*
  *Don't worry about dinner for tonight. We'll cook it **ourselves**.*
  *Can the twins dress **themselves** yet, or are they still too young?*

- The reflexive pronoun ends in *self* or *selves*.

I	**myself**	We	**ourselves**
You	**yourself**	You (pl.)	**yourselves**
He	**himself**		
She	**herself**	They	**themselves**
It	**itself**		

Unit 25

Nondefining relative clauses

- Use nondefining relative clauses to add extra information to a sentence. The sentence would make sense without the nondefining relative clause.
  My car needs service.
  *My car, **which is two years old**, needs service.*
  My pet rabbit died in June.
  *My pet rabbit, **who was adorable**, died in June.*

- Introduce nondefining relative clauses with **who, whose, where, when**, and **which**, but not **that**.
  *Kate Moss, **who is an international model**, bought one of the T-shirts.*
  *Arezzo, **which isn't very far from Siena**, is an interesting town.*

- In formal situations, the relative pronoun **whom** is used instead of **who** when it is in object position.
  *My friend Mike, **whom** I met in college, lives next door to me.*

Note: Use commas before and after nondefining relative clauses.

Unit 26

Past unreal conditional and *I wish/If only*

- Form the past unreal conditional with
  If + **subject** + **had/hadn't** + **the past participle**, **subject** + **would/wouldn't** + **have** + **the past participle**
  ***If I had waited** for the sale, **I wouldn't have paid** so much for the shirt.*

- Use the past unreal conditional to talk about how things might have been different in the past. Past unreal conditional sentences can express regret, relief, and accusations.
  ***If I hadn't bought** the hat, **I wouldn't have felt** so stupid.*
  (But I did buy the hat, and I did feel stupid.)
  ***If they had phoned** us, **they would have found out** we needed help.*
  (But they didn't phone, so they didn't find out.)

- You can also use **I wish I had/hadn't** + **the past participle** and **If only I had/hadn't** + **the past participle** to express regret.
  ***I wish I had gone** to bed earlier!* (But I didn't.)
  ***If only I hadn't gone** to bed so late!* (But I did.)

Note: When the *if* **clause** goes first, put a comma after it. You don't need a comma when it goes at the end.
__If__ I hadn't been so late, I'd have seen the movie.
I'd have seen the movie __if__ I hadn't been so late.

Unit 27

Verb + infinitive, verb + gerund, and preposition + gerund
(See also Unit 17.)

- **Use the infinitive after certain verbs** such as *agree, appear, arrange, choose, expect, hope, manage, offer, plan, pretend, promise, refuse, seem, threaten, try.*
  *She **plans to take** a computer course.*
  *He **expects to get** a raise.*
  *My children **refuse to eat** vegetables.*

- **Use the gerund after certain verbs and verb phrases** such as ***avoid, can't help, discuss, dislike, enjoy, finish, imagine, mention, (don't) mind, miss, postpone, quit, regret, suggest.***
  *I **can't help worrying** about the kids when they stay out late.*
  *I **don't mind doing** the laundry, but I really **dislike vacuuming**.*
  *We **avoid taking** the train during rush hour because it's so crowded.*

- **Use either the infinitive or gerund after certain verbs and verb phrases** such as *begin, can't stand, continue, hate, like, love, start.*
  *He **started talking/to talk** when he was one year old.*
  *She **loves to go/going** for long walks.*
  *I **can't stand getting up/to get up** early in the morning.*

- Use the gerund after a preposition.
  *She's looking forward **to going** away to college.*
  *He knew what was in the letter **without reading** it.*
  *Why don't we have dinner at home **instead of eating** out?*

Note: *To* is a preposition, not part of the infinitive form, in **look forward to**, so a gerund follows it.

Unit 28

Past modals for deduction

- Use ***must have*** + **the past participle** when you are almost sure something was true.
  *She **must have been** a storyteller.*
  (I am almost sure she was a storyteller.)

- Use ***might have*** + **the past participle**, ***may have*** + **the past participle**, or ***could have*** + **the past participle** when you think something was possible.
  *She **might have had** extra food because of her status.*
  *She **may have been** a storyteller.*
  *She **could have been** a religious figure.*
  (But I'm not sure.)

- Use ***can't have*** + **the past participle** when you are sure something wasn't true.
  *Silk **can't have come** from the area they lived in.*
  (I am sure that silk didn't come from the area they lived in.)

Note: Use modals to make deductions about things in the present, too.

- Use ***must*** + **the base form** when you are almost sure something is true.
  *That **must be** an insect—it's got six legs.*

- Use ***can't*** + **the base form** when you are almost sure something isn't true.
  *That **can't be** a spider. It has only six legs. Spiders have eight legs.*

- Use ***might*** (or ***may*** or ***could***) + **the base form** when you think something is possible.
  *I think it **might be** a bee.*

Irregular Verbs

Base form	Simple past / Past participle / Present participle	Base form	Simple past / Past participle / Present participle
be	was (were) / been / being	know	knew / known / knowing
become	became / become / becoming	leave	left / left / leaving
begin	began / begun / beginning	lose	lost / lost / losing
break	broke / broken / breaking	make	made / made / making
bring	brought / brought / bringing	mean	meant / meant / meaning
build	built / built / building	meet	met / met / meeting
buy	bought / bought / buying	put	put / put / putting
catch	caught / caught / catching	read	read / read / reading
choose	chose / chosen / choosing	ride	rode / ridden / riding
come	came / come / coming	run	ran / run / running
do	did / done / doing	say	said / said / saying
drink	drank / drunk / drinking	see	saw / seen / seeing
drive	drove / driven / driving	sell	sold / sold / selling
eat	ate / eaten / eating	show	showed / shown / showing
fall	fell / fallen / falling	sit	sat / sat / sitting
find	found / found / finding	speak	spoke / spoken / speaking
fly	flew / flown / flying	spend	spent / spent / spending
forget	forgot / forgotten / forgetting	take	took / taken / taking
get	got / gotten / getting	tell	told / told / telling
give	gave / given / giving	think	thought / thought / thinking
go	went / gone / going	throw	threw / thrown / throwing
grow	grew / grown / growing	understand	understood / understood /understanding
have	had / had / having	wear	wore / worn / wearing
hear	heard / heard / hearing	win	won / won / winning
keep	kept / kept / keeping	write	wrote / written / writing

Vocabulary

Unit 1
clutter
contentment
energy
good health
good luck
happiness
productivity
stress
success
tension
tranquility
wealth

Unit 2
first-aid kit
hiking boots
insect repellent
money belt
rain gear
sleeping bag
travel guide
water bottle

Unit 3
basil
beer
butter
onions
pepper
salt
shrimp
stock

chili powder
garlic
ground beef
kidney beans
tomatoes
tomato paste
vegetable oil

add
(bring to a) boil
broil
chop
melt
mix
pour
sauté
serve
simmer
soak
stir

Unit 4
action figure
board game
cards
doll
erector set truck
handheld video game
jigsaw puzzle
remote-controlled car
skateboard
stuffed animal

Unit 5
blow your nose
eat with your fingers
have your elbows on the
    table
point at someone
put your feet up on the
    chair
reach across the table
slurp while eating
snap your fingers

Unit 6
achieve a goal/an objective
come up with an idea/a
    solution
develop a skill/a plan
invent a machine/a device
overcome an obstacle/a
    problem
pass an exam/a course
receive a certificate/an
    award
solve a problem/a puzzle
win a race/a prize

Unit 7
be accused of something
be convicted of something
be suspected of something
check on something or
    someone
commit a crime
deter someone
eavesdrop on someone
get away with something
keep an eye on something
    or someone
keep tabs on someone
look at something or
    someone

protect someone
restrict something
spy on someone
take advantage of
    something
uncover something

Unit 8
baggage claim
boarding pass
carry-on bag
check-in counter
duty-free shops
flight attendant
gate
luggage
runway
security checkpoint

Unit 9
cloud cover
clouds
fog
rain
showers
snow
sunshine
thunderstorms
tornado
winds

Unit 10
climb
decline
decrease
deteriorate
drop
fall
get better
get worse
go down
go up
improve
increase
rise
strengthen
weaken
worsen

Unit 11
experience
long-term goals
promotion
prospects

qualifications
references
strengths
weaknesses

Unit 12
afterward
at the same time
earlier
every time
previously
simultaneously
subsequently
whenever

Unit 13
cut off
fearful
isolated
jittery
jumpy
lonesome
petrified
scared
solitary
stressed out
tense
terrified

Unit 14
by the time
do something on time
in time for something
leisure time
a matter of time
spend time somewhere or
    with someone
take a long time
time off
a waste of time

Unit 15
bore someone to tears
brag about something
chat about something
complain about something
confide in someone
gossip
make small talk
talk about someone behind
    his or her back

Unit 16

Adjectives | **Nouns**
fashionable | fashion
influential | influence
mediocre | mediocrity
popular | popularity
sensational | sensation
spectacular | spectacle
successful | success
talented | talent
trendy | trend

Unit 17

cold cuts
a dish
fish
ingredients
a meal
meat
a recipe
seafood
snacks
takeout

Unit 18

authorities
cell
guards
life sentence
political prisoner
prisoner
privilege
supervision

Unit 19

an anthology
a best-seller
a biography
a column
an encyclopedia
a manual
a novel
poetry/poems
a textbook

Unit 20

hearing
sight
smell
taste
touch

feel (adjective)
feel like something
look (adjective)
look like something
smell (adjective)
smell like something
sound (adjective)
sound like something
taste (adjective)
taste like something

Unit 21

bait and switch
coupons
exaggeration
fine print
loss leader
out of stock
package deal
rebate
warranty

Unit 22

consult with someone
do business somewhere or with
    someone
exchange business cards
go on business trips
make contact
negotiate a deal
reach an agreement
schedule a meeting
set up an appointment
take risks

Unit 23

adolescent
adult
child
kid
teenager
toddler
senior citizen

bring up someone
count on someone
get away with something
grow up
look forward to
look up to someone
make up something
pick on someone
think over something

Unit 24

cater a party
deliver the newspaper
do the shopping/the housework/
    the ironing/the cooking/the dishes
fix a pipe
make the beds
organize closets
repair the car
serve the food

Unit 25

Nouns | **Verbs**
an ad/advertisement | advertise
a business | do business
a design | design
a market | market
a plan | plan
a product | produce
a profit | make a profit

Unit 26

bargain
clearance sale
haggling
on impulse
a refund
shop around
take things back
try clothes on
vendors
window shopping

Unit 27

bitter
cheerful
cynical
easygoing
glum
level-headed
optimistic
pessimistic
short-tempered
sociable

Unit 28

ancestor
culture
customs
generation
status
society
traditions
tribe

Acknowledgments

The authors and series editor wish to acknowledge with gratitude the following reviewers, consultants, and piloters for their thoughtful contributions to the development of *WorldView*.

BRAZIL: São Paulo: Sérgio Gabriel, **FMU/Cultura Inglesa, Jundiaí;** Heloísa Helena Medeiros Ramos, **Kiddy and Teen;** Zaina Nunes, Márcia Mathias Pinto, Angelita Goulvea Quevedo, **Pontifícia Universidade Católica;** Rosa Laquimia Souza, **FMU-FIAM;** Élcio Camilo Alves de Souza, Marie Adele Ryan, **Associação Alumni;** Maria Antonieta Gagliardi, **Centro Britânico;** Chris Ritchie, Debora Schisler, Sandra Natalini, **Sevenidiomas;** Joacyr Oliveira, **FMU;** Maria Thereza Garrelhas Gentil, **Colégio Mackenzie;** Carlos Renato Lopes, **Uni-Santana;** Yara M. Bannwart Rago, **Associação Escola Graduada de São Paulo;** Jacqueline Zilberman, **Instituto King's Cross;** Vera Lúcia Cardoso Berk, **Talkative Idioms Center;** Ana Paula Hoepers, **Instituto Winners;** Carlos C.S. de Celis, Daniel Martins Neto, **CEL-LEP;** Maria Carmen Castellani, **União Cultural Brasil Estados Unidos;** Kátia Martins P. de Moraes Leme, **Colégio Pueri Domus;** Luciene Martins Farias, **Aliança Brasil Estados Unidos;** Neide Aparecida Silva, **Cultura Inglesa;** Áurea Shinto, **Santos:** Maria Lúcia Bastos, **Instituto Four Seasons.**
CANADA: Stella Waterman, **Camosun College.**
COLOMBIA: Bogota: Sergio Monguí, Rafael Díaz Morales, **Universidad de la Salle;** Yecid Ortega Páez, Yojanna Ruiz G., **Universidad Javeriana;** Merry García Metzger, **Universidad Minuto de Dios;** Maria Caterina Barbosa, **Coninglés;** Nelson Martínez R., **Asesorías Académicas;** Eduardo Martínez, Stella Lozano Vega, **Universidad Santo Tomás de Aquino;** Kenneth McIntyre, **ABC English Institute. JAPAN: Tokyo:** Peter Bellars, **Obirin University;** Michael Kenning, **Takushoku University;** Martin Meldrum, **Takushoku University;** Carol Ann Moritz, **New International School;** Mary Sandkamp, **Musashi Sakai;** Dan Thompson, **Yachiyo Chiba-ken/American Language Institute;** Carol Vaughn, **Kanto Kokusai High School. Osaka:** Lance Burrows, **Osaka Prefecture Settsu High School;** Bonnie Carpenter, **Mukogawa Joshi Daigaku/ Hannan Daigaku;** Josh Glaser, Richard Roy, **Human International University/Osaka Jogakuin Junior College;** Gregg Kennerly, **Osaka YMCA;** Ted Ostis, **Otemon University;** Chris Page, **ECC Language Institute;** Leon Pinsky, **Kwansei Gakuin University;** Chris Ruddenklau, **Kinki University;** John Smith, **Osaka International University. Saitama:** Marie Cosgrove, **Surugadai University. Kobe:** Donna Fujimoto, **Kobe University of Commerce.**
KOREA: Seoul: Adrienne Edwards-Daugherty, Min Hee Kang, James Kirkmeyer, Paula Reynolds, Warren Weappa, Matthew Williams, **YBM ELS Shinchon;** Brian Cook, Jack Scott, Russell Tandy, **Hanseoung College. MEXICO: Mexico City:** Alberto Hern, **Instituto Anglo Americano de Idiomas;** Eugenia Carbonell, **Universidad Interamericana;** Cecilia Rey Gutiérrez, María del Rosario Escalada Ruiz, **Universidad Motolinia;** Salvador Castañeda, Alan Bond, Eduardo Fernández, Carla Silva, **Universidad Panamericana;** Raquel Márquez Colin, **Universidad St. John's;** Francisco Castillo, Carlos René Malacara Ramos, **CELE – UNAM/Mascarones;** Belem Saint Martin, **Preparatoria ISEC;** María Guadalupe Aguirre Hernández, **Comunidad Educativa Montessori;** Isel Vargas Ruelas, Patricia Contreras, **Centro Universitario Oparin;** Gabriela Juárez Hernández, Arturo Vergara Esteban Juan, **English Fast Center;** Jesús Armando Martínez Salgado, **Preparatoria Leon Tolstoi;** Regina Peña Martínez, **Centro Escolar Anahuac;** Guadalupe Buenrostro, **Colegio Partenon;** Rosendo Rivera Sánchez, **Colegio Anglo Español;** María Rosario Hernández Reyes, **Escuela Preparatoria Monte Albán;** Fernanda Cruzado, **Instituto Tecnológico del Sur;** Janet Harris M., **Colegio Anglo Español;** Rosalba Pérez Contreras, **Centro Lingüístico Empresarial. Ecatepec:** Diana Patricia Ordaz García, **Comunidad Educativa Montessori;** Leticia Ricart P., **Colegio Holandés;** Samuel Hernández B., **Instituto Cultural Renacimiento. Tlalpan:** Ana María Cortés, **Centro Educativo José P. Cacho. San Luis Potosí:** Sigi Orta Hernández, María de Guadalupe Barrientos J., **Instituto Hispano Inglés;** Antonieta Raya Z., **Instituto Potosino;** Gloria Carpizo, **Seminario Mayor Arquidiocesano de San Luis Potosí;** Susana Prieto Noyola, Silvia Yolanda Ortiz Romo, **Universidad Politécnica de San Luis Potosí;** Rosa Arrendondo Flores, **Instituto Potosino/Universidad Champagnat;** María Cristina Carmillo, María Carmen García Leos, **Departamento Universitario de Inglés, UASLP;** María Gloria Candia Castro, **Universidad Tecnológica SLP;** Bertha Guadalupe Garza Treviño, **Centro de Idiomas, UASLP. Guadalajara:** Nancy Patricia Gómez Ley, **Escuela Técnica Palmares;** Gabriela Michel Vázquez, Jim Nixon, **Colegio Cervantes Costa Rica;** Abraham Barbosa Martínez, Lucía Huerta Cervantes, Paulina Cervantes Fernández, Audrey Lizaola López, **Colegio Enrique de Osso;** Ana Cristina Plascencia Haro, Joaquín Limón Ramos, **Centro Educativo Tlaquepaque III;** Rocío de Miguel, **Colegio La Paz;** Hilda Delgado Parga, **Colegio D'Monaco;** Claudia Rodríguez, **English Key. León:** Laura Montes de la Serna, **Colegio Británico A.C.;** Antoinette Marie Hernández, **"The Place 4U2 Learn" Language School;** Delia Zavala Torres, Verónica Medellín Urbina, **EPCA Sur;** María Eugenia Gutiérrez Mena, Ana Paulina Suárez Cervantes, **Universidad la Salle;** Herlinda Rodríguez Hernández, **Instituto Mundo Verde;** María Rosario Torres Neri, **Instituto Jassa. Aguascalientes:** María Teresa Robles Cázares, **Escuela de la Ciudad de Aguascalientes / Universidad de Aguascalientes;** María Dolores Jiménez Chávez, **ECA – Universidad Autónoma de Aguascalientes;** María Aguirre Hernández, **ECA – Proyecto Start;** Fernando Xavier Gómez Orenday, **UAA – IEA "Keep On";** Felisia Guadalupe García Ruiz, **Universidad Tecnológica;** Margarita Zapiain B., **Universidad Autónoma de Aguascalientes;** Martha Ayala Cardoza, **Universidad de la Concordia / Escuela de la Ciudad de Aguascalientes;** Gloria Aguirre Hernández, **Escuela de la Ciudad de Aguascalientes;** Hector Arturo Moreno Díaz, **Universidad Bonaterra.**